This book is due for return on or before the last date shown below.

About the Author:

Peter Davies a co-editor on this series is a former lecturer in English a skilled and experienced writer, the author of serveral forthcoming titles in this series, including W.B. Yeats.

Greenwich Exchange

First published in Great Britain in 1996

William Blake © Peter Davies, 19965
All rights reserved

Printed and bound by Priory Press, Holywood, N. Ireland.

ISBN 1-871551-27-7

CONTENTS

CHRONOLOGY

1757   28th November, born at 28 Broad Street, Soho, London.

1767   Entered Henry Pars's drawing school in the Strand.

1769   Begins writing the poems that will be published as the *Poetical Sketches* in 1783.

1772   Becomes apprenticed to the engraver James Basire, for whom he will work for the next seven years.

1773   Date of his first known engraving, *Joseph of Arimathea among the Rocks of Albion.*

1774   The tomb of Edward I in Westminster Abbey opened. Blake makes sketches of the body in the coffin.

1779   Admitted to the Royal Academy Schools. Fellow students include John Flaxman and Thomas Stothard.

1780   Exhibits *The Death of Earl Godwin* at the Royal Academy. Is caught up in the mob that liberates Newgate Prison. Commissioned to do engravings by Joseph Johnson.

1782   Marries Catherine Boucher. They set up home at 23 Green Street, Leicester Fields.

1783   Is introduced by Flaxman into the Mathew set. The Rev A. S. Mathew finances the printing of his *Poetical Sketches.*

1784   Blake's father dies. Probable date of composition of the satire on the Mathew circle, *An Island in the Moon.*

1787   Blake's younger and favourite brother Robert dies.

1789   *Tiriel,* the *Songs of Innocence* and *The Book of Thel.*

1790   Moves to Hercules Buildings, Lambeth.

1791   *The French Revolution* printed by Johnson. Remains in page proof.

1793   *The Marriage of Heaven and Hell, Visions of the Daughters of Albion* and *America*.

1794   *The Songs of Innocence and Experience, Europe* and *The Book of Urizen*.

1795. *The Song of Los, The Book of Ahania* and *The Book of Los*.

1799   Blake benefits for the first time from the patronage of Thomas Butts.

1800. Executes three engravings for William Hayley's *Essay on Sculpture* (June). Moves to Felpham, Sussex, to be under Hayley's patronage (September).

1802   First series of Hayley's *Ballads* with illustrations by Blake.

1803   First two volumes of Hayley's *Life of William Cowper*, with illustrations by Blake. On 12th August Blake ejects the soldier William Scofield from his garden. Scofield lays a charge of sedition against him.
       In September Blake and Catherine return to London.

1804. 11th January, acquitted of sedition at Chichester.

1806   Benjamin Heath Malkin's *A Father's Memoirs of his Child*; contains a biographical sketch of Blake.

1808   Blair's *The Grave* with Blake's designs engraved by Schiavonetti. Annotations to Sir Joshua Reynolds's *Discourses*. *Milton*, on which Blake has been working since 1804, is engraved.

1809. Blake's exhibition of his work at his brother James's Broad Street hosier's shop is a complete failure. It contains his painting of Chaucer's pilgrims, the idea for which he believes Stothard has 'stolen' from him.

1811   Henry Crabb Robinson's critical essay on Blake, with translations into German of some of the *Songs*, published in the Hamburg periodical *Vaterländisches Museum*.

1818   Coleridge reads and praises *Songs of Innocence and Experience*. Blake meets his last patron, the young painter John Linnell.

1820.   *Jerusalem*, on which Blake had been at work since 1804, is completed.

1821   Moves to his last home, 3 Fountain Court, Strand.

1824   Is introduced to Samuel Palmer while working on his illustrations to Dante, a series left unfinished at his death.

1825   The engravings to the Book of Job completed.

1826   In *The Plain Speaker* Hazlitt includes Blake in a list of 'profound mystics'.

1827   On 12th August Blake dies at Fountain Court. In September Catherine goes to live with Linnell as his housekeeper.

1830   An entry on Blake in Cunningham's *Lives of the Most Eminent British Painters*.

1831   Catherine Blake retires to lodgings where she dies on 18th October.

1863   First edition of Alexander Gilchrist's *Life of William Blake*.

1 PERSPECTIVE

When William Blake died in 1827 he was unacknowledged as meriting a place in the history of literature or graphic art. True, there were those few who had *en passant* discerned his genius. Among them were literary figures of the stature of Coleridge, Hazlitt and Lamb, and painters such as Henry Fuseli and Samuel Palmer. But they were so few, and their glance had alighted so cursorily on him that the effect of their acknowledgement was negligible. In terms of his possible artistic development it was certainly far too late to help him. Blake's resolute sense of being an isolated figure in the world, tended to ensure that, for his time at least, his integrity would have to be its own reward.

The place Blake occupies in English literature today is still as a solitary and unique figure. The body of his work is so sprawling, diverse and frequently so difficult of access that it cannot be any accident that we are so often asked, even by his most fervent apologists, to judge him as a seer or mystic rather than as a poet. By the same token, his performance as a graphic artist sometimes seems to need special pleading. He cannot be placed directly alongside his rough contemporaries Turner and Constable, or even a much more kindred spirit like Samuel Palmer, without an appeal to qualities other than those of the purely visual. When we approach his pictures we are often asked to see, as he did, with the inner eye. We are required to be aware, in advance, of the religious philosophy behind the graphic result.

If Blake is to be considered among the Romantic poets, it has to be understood that, unique among them, he had a consistent religious belief. His mysticism is not, like that of Wordsworth, a question of dimly-sensed supernatural forces emanating from the countryside in which he moves. To Blake, the spiritual world is as familiar and as clearly delineated as it was to the mystics of the Middle Ages. Among the Romantic painters, too, he stands apart through his complete refusal not only to paint landscape, but to paint from life at all. He does not, like Palmer, depict extant natural forms and then imbue them

1

with spiritual significance. His pictures are, rather, emblems of inner and eternal conflicts as he envisions them.

There is little point in trying to pretend that the long prophetic books do not present difficulties to the reader. The question is whether they are, as in Mona Wilson's estimate, "terrific crags" which yield few riches for much toil, or whether, as Northrop Frye thinks, they are a "normal adaptation of the language of poetry" and that therefore in any estimation of Blake "the longer and more difficult prophecies will have to bear the weight of the commentary".

If the first is the case, we have to ask whether it was Blake's increasing isolation that produced the obscurities of the later work, or whether he possessed a didactic streak which, in spite of himself, operated increasingly against his poetic inspiration. The very thought would have horrified a man who created the Jehovah/Satan figure Urizen (from the Greek ὁpιzειv: to set boundaries, to limit), the controller and circumscriber of human thought and action.

And if Northrop Frye, David Erdman and later commentators are right in their judgement that the language of the prophetic books is consistent with that of the rest of Blake's output, then we must wonder how it was that a man who could distil such a concentration of thought and experience in a lyric line like:

O Rose, thou art sick!

could also ask us to accept this (from the mouth of Blake's Satan in *Jerusalem*) as poetry:

I am your Rational Power, O Albion, & that Human Form
You call Divine is but a Worm seventy inches long
That creeps forth in a night & is dried in the morning sun,
In fortuitous concourse of Memorys accumulated and lost...

or that a man who produced the potent aphorism "The tygers of wrath are wiser than the horses of instruction" could later descend to the tetchy narrowness of "Where any view of Money exists, Art cannot be carried on".

But these are reservations that must be faced later. For the fact is that if in any one of the spheres in which he moved: the lyric poem;

2

the symbolic epic; the prose epigram; the letter; painting and engraving, Blake has his peers, his performance in the sum of these activities reveals a figure of such vitality and force that from the obscurity of 150 years ago he has come to occupy an unassailable position in English literature and visual art.

In his celebrated essay *Culture and Anarchy* of 1869, Matthew Arnold defined two strands in British culture which he saw as being almost always at war with each other. He called them (following Heine) Hebraism and Hellenism - "strictness of conscience" and "spontaneity of consciousness". Arnold's tract is, to a degree, a plea for the release of 19th-century English culture and society from what he saw as the dominant puritanical tendencies of the first, while insisting on its undoubted strengths. To Blake, writing three generations before Arnold, the notion of spontaneity of consciousness is paramount. It is the central theme of that series of aphorisms he was provocatively to entitle Proverbs of Hell. For Blake, "He who desires but acts not, breeds pestilence", and the Tygers of Wrath are always to be preferred to the Horses of Instruction. But unlike Arnold, a Victorian gentleman whose very position as Inspector of Schools would have prevented him from being detected, as Blake was, sitting naked in his garden with his wife, a freedom from the dictates of conscience is not merely a social and cultural matter. For Blake it is the basis of the entire mental and spiritual universe, which Man will ultimately share, on equal footing, with God.

2 CHILDHOOD AND YOUTH

William Blake was born at Broad Street in London's Soho on 28th November 1757. An early school of critics, headed, understandably enough, by Yeats, ascribes Irish ancestry to him. This school gives him a grandfather called O'Neil who romantically escapes debt by marrying Blake's grandmother, the keeper apparently of a Dublin shebeen. This is represented as an act of redemption, though how the proprietress of an illicit liquor store accomplished that is not specified. At any rate, O'Neil took his wife's name, as did his illegitimate son of a previous liaison, who subsequently married and settled in London, to become Blake's father.

To a larger group - and one of more persistent tendencies - Blake is a "Cockney" which, so we are told, explains a good deal about his later falling out with with Hayley and rural Felpham. There is scarcely any more validity in the Cockney description than there is in the Irish fairy tale. The Irish story has the merit of charm - but not one scrap of documentary evidence to substantiate it. It overlooks, too, the fact that in his own eyes William Blake was always "English Blake".

The term Cockney is equally mischievous when applied to a man like Blake. For a start, his Soho birthplace is manifestly not within the prescribed sound of Bow Bells. Moreover, with its contemporary implications of streetwise cunning, bred on the pavements of an amorphous metropolis, the Cockney notion is clearly not relevant to the mid-Georgian London into which Blake was born. London life then was not "urban" as we have come to think of the word. There was pasture land not so far to the north of what is now Oxford Street and a little to the west of modern Bond Street. To the south of the Thames, apart from the modestly built-up areas of Rotherhithe and Southwark, open country stretched away virtually from the shingle and mud foreshore to the North Downs. Lambeth, where Blake was subsequently to describe himself as "giving his body ease/......beneath the poplar trees" (i.e. defaecating, something he could hardly have done on a riverside esplanade) had not long before been a marsh.

This has not deterred Northrop Frye for whom: "Blake was, like most major English writers, a born Cockney who quickly became miserable long outside London". While for a more recent entry to the ranks of Blake commentators, Peter Ackroyd, "He was a Cockney visionary".

Both Blake's parents were Dissenters. But how vigorously and in what manner their dissent was practised is not clear. Evidently neither of them were remotely cranky. There seems to have been no attempt to force-feed their children with religious ideas. Indeed, from the outset Mrs Blake appears to have been thoroughly alarmed by the extreme spirituality of her son. Notions that Blake was brought up in a hotbed of Swedenborgianism have, too, long since been dispelled. Swedenborg did not come to London until 1771 and died there in 1772. His *Heaven and Hell* and other works were not translated into English until towards the end of the 1780s, by which time Blake was intellectually mature. All that can be said with certainty is that from the educational point of view Blake's father adopted a commendably liberal attitude to William's remarkable propensities. He was not made to go to school, but left to pursue his tastes in reading and art much as he pleased. Of his brothers, only the eldest, James, and his favourite, Robert, who died young, impinge much on his life. There was also a sister, Catherine.

We know little that is specific of Blake's early studies. Clearly he had read Spenser, Shakespeare, other Elizabethans and Milton. Nearer his own period, Akenside, Macpherson's *Ossian*, Piercey's *Reliques* and, later, Chatterton were among the material available to him. But it is unprofitable to try to ascribe particular sources to such a singular creativity as the young Blake's was.

From an early age he was a solitary individual. He frequently went for long walks which might take him over one of the Thames bridges to ramble in the Surrey countryside. In the mid-18th century on June days hay was mowed not far south of the riverbank. In those hayfields, famously, at the age of eight he once saw a tree swarming with angels. It was far from being his only childhood contact with the spiritual world. When much younger, he had been frightened by the appearance of God at a window. Later he told his mother that he had seen Ezekiel on one of his rambles. Whatever the religious notions current in the Blake household, such spiritual precocity was not part of them. William's visions alarmed Mrs Blake who rebuked him and advised him, on pain of more severe chastisement, not to let his father hear of such things.

This childlike assurance of the validity of his visions is central to Blake's personality and creative impulses. To the end of his life he was to retain it undimmed. The spiritual world was a concrete reality to him. He saw it as clearly as the Virgin Mary in Fra Angelico's *Annunciation* sees the Angel Gabriel, or as St Teresa of Avila saw the devil that pursued her. It was an apprehension of the spiritual world quite unlike the cloudy mysteries sometimes perpetrated by the later Romantics. The meditative exercises through which a mediaeval mystic sought to bring himself to a direct contemplation of the divine were totally unnecessary to Blake. In a moment - one generally completely unsought by himself - he was able to cross the divide between the world of physical reality and that of the spirit. For him, the latter was simply the next room.

His earliest impetus to artistic self-expression was through drawing rather than writing (and to graphic art he was to return at the end of his life, when the world had rejected him). His father, realising that his energies needed some conduit, sent him to a drawing school in the Strand. He also encouraged him by buying him copies of the sculptures that were then familar, the *Farnese Hercules* and the *Venus de Medici*. His artistic taste was further formed by prints of Michelangelo and Albrecht Dürer, whom he was to revere for the rest of his life. They gave him his ideas of what was artistically "right" from a very early age. When he later came into contact with the riotous style of Rubens he pronounced it to be anathema.

When Blake had finished at the drawing school, his father intended that he should learn painting at a private studio. William dissented from this on the grounds that the high fees would have damaged his brothers' educational opportunities. Instead, at 14 he was apprenticed to an engraver, James Basire. Thus he learned the trade which was always to give him the means of earning at least a crust. It was also to give the world one of the most splendid manifestations of his graphic powers when, towards the end of his life, he used it to produce his magnificent *Vision of the Book of Job*.

Few men can claim to have exerted much influence on Blake. But to Basire, who was evidently a fine craftsman, a kind master and a good man, belongs the credit of having imparted to his pupil a thorough mastery of his craft. Wisely, he taught him the technical essentials without attempting to influence his notions of design.

A harmonious relationship grew up between master and pupil which continued for two years. Then there was a hiccup. Basire took on two more apprentices. What happened at that point is not completely clear. There appears to have been some youthful mischief making, a boyish ganging-up and taking of sides. A complete innocent in the world of schoolboy politicking, Blake seems to have taken the part of the unruly new recruits against his master. At any rate, Basire had the wisdom not to make an issue of the matter. He sent Blake off to Westminster Abbey to make drawings of the tombs and other monuments.

This was a decisive step in Blake's development. Hours of solitude among the solemn memorials of a far-off age made a profound impression on his imagination. They gave him a vision of the Middle Ages and, as he saw it, the further past stretching back to the dawn of Christianity and into the heart of eternity. Among the pencil sketches he executed at that period are the effigies of King Henry II and Queen Eleanor. He was also present, in May 1774, at the occasion of that interesting piece of antiquarian sacrilege, the opening of the tomb of of King Edward I, and made several rough sketches of it.

From this period comes a characteristic work, *Joseph of Arimathea among the Rocks of Albion*, which Blake engraved in 1773 at the age of 16. Joseph is a solid, almost massive, figure. The handling already shows the influence of Michelangelo, on whose *Crucifixion of St Peter*

7

in the Vatican it is based. It is a competent, rather than inspired, image. Nevertheless it is the prototype of many of Blake's later figures. The legend was added in a later engraving. But it indicates Blake's preoccupation with the Gothic (as he saw it) and his complete disregard for a historically exact approach to the evolution of Christianity.

This is One of the Gothic Artists who built the Cathedrals in what we call the Dark Ages, wandering about in sheepskins and goatskins; of whom the World was not worthy. Such were the Christians in all Ages.

For Blake, the true Christian - indeed Christ himself - is an artist, and the practice of the Christian faith is always to be the same thing as the practice of art. Worship is to be a mental, not devotional, activity. The Christian must never "cease from mental fight", as he was later to sing in the famously misnamed "Jerusalem" poem which begins his symbolic work *Milton*.

Meanwhile, Blake had been writing. Although the *Poetical Sketches* were not collected and printed until 1783, they are described in the Rev A. S. Mathew's preface to them as having been written between the ages of 12 and 20, in other words between 1769 and 1777. At the latter date Dr Johnson still has seven years to live; Wordsworth's *Descriptive Sketches* are fifteen years away.

We do not know at what age any one of the *Poetical Sketches* was composed. The collection opens with the remarkable offering "To Spring". It seems reasonable to assume it is one of the earliest poems Blake wrote.

O thou with dewy locks, who lookest down
Thro' the clear windows of the morning, turn
Thine angel eyes upon our western isle,
Which in full choir hails thy approach, O Spring!

The hills tell each other, and the list'ning
Vallies hear; all our longing eyes are turned
Up to thy bright pavillions: issue forth,
And let thy holy feet visit our clime.

Come o'er the eastern hills, and let our winds
Kiss thy perfumed garments; let us taste
Thy morn and evening breath; scatter thy pearls
Upon our lovesick land that mourns for thee.

> O deck her forth with thy fair fingers; pour
> Thy soft kisses on her bosom; and put
> Thy golden crown upon thy languish'd head,
> Whose modest tresses were bound up for thee!

What is extraordinary about this performance is that it feels not like the work of a juvenile, but of a poet in the full enjoyment of his powers. There is nothing prentice, tentative or imitative about it. Granted there are echoes in it of Milton and Akenside. Other poems throughout the collection nod towards Spenser, Shakespeare, Milton, Gray and the gothicising poets Blake had read. But the influences are fully assimilated. If we approach any of these lyrics with the feeling that it perhaps "reminds" us of something Shakespearean or Miltonic, that feeling is soon dispelled by the sensation of being in the presence of an original sensibility using apparently familiar material in a completely individual manner.

The freedom with which the verse in these four quatrains is handled is striking. It is the verse of a man imbued with confidence in what he is doing. Rhyme and the end-stopped line, those disciplinary lifelines of the apprentice, have been totally jettisoned. Meaning is allowed to flow down through each stanza. Lines like:

> Come o'er the Eastern hills and let our winds
> Kiss thy perfumed garments; let us taste
> Thy morning and evening breath...

have the kind of poetic life we associate with that of a late Shakespeare play. At moments, daring rhythmical changes almost threaten to break the mould of the individual quatrains:

> ....pour
> Thy soft kisses on her bosom; and put
> Thy golden crown..........

But they never quite do. And the mastery of the performance is sealed in the triumphant cadence of ther final line:

> Whose modest tresses were bound up for thee.

From the point of view purely of verse writing, then, this is an assured, almost virtuoso, debut. But the content is no less remarkable than the technique. The opening line "O thou whose dewy locks..." may use a familiar enough epithet from the Elizabethan/Jacobean poetic armoury. But what follows is something very different from a stock invocation to Spring. By the second stanza we are confronted by something which is entirely Blakean:

> .....all our longing eyes are turned
> Up to thy bright pavillions: issue forth,
> And let thy holy feet visit our clime.

This has gone far beyond pure nature poetry. It is ecstatic and inspirational. It is, already, palpably the language of the man who could later write "And did those feet in ancient time".

We have only to compare it with the verse of Wordsworth's "An Evening Walk" to see the difference. The latter was printed in 1793, though probably composed between 1787 and 1789. Like the later poems of the *Poetical Sketches*, then, it is a performance of the late teens.

> Where silver rocks the savage prospect chear
> Of giant yews that frown on Rydale's mere;
> Where peace to Grasmere's lonely island leads,
> To willowy hedgerows and to emerald meads;
> Leads to her bridge, rude church and cottag'd grounds,
> Her rocky sheepwalks, and her woodland bounds;

In Wordsworth's poem the images "savage prospect", "emerald meads", and "rude church" have no function that would not have been thoroughly familiar to any tolerably well-versed poetaster of the previous three or four generations.

Writing a dozen years after Blake, the young Wordsworth is still firmly entrenched in the poetic diction and habits of mind of the 18th century. He is a quantum leap from the verse and perceptions of the *Lyrical Ballads* and *The Prelude*. In the *Poetical Sketches* Blake has, by comparison, risen completely above the formalism of his age.

"To Spring" is discussed at this length not because it this the most remarkable of the poems which make up the *Poetical Sketches* (others could have been chosen to make the point with much greater force) but simply because it is the first the reader encounters on opening Blake's complete writings. It is the first, too, of what might easily in a young poet have been a series of conventional invocations to the seasons, but are, in fact, something else. In all of them Blake gives the impression not merely of having escaped from the shackles of Augustan poetic conventions, but of being completely unable to utilise them for his creative purposes.

"To the Evening Star" is a treatment of a familiar theme which is as different from that of Collins's much earlier "Ode to Evening" as can be imagined. The Collins poem is in the pastoral tradition - and of the genre it is exquisite. (By comparison Blake's is somewhat rough-hewn.) For Collins the presiding genius of that time of the day is a "Nymph reserv'd", a "calm Vot'ress" and the evening star itself is a "paly circlet". The poem is a passive meditation on a time of quiet. Blake's evening star is by comparison a thing of energy. Its "bright torch of love" can be invoked to protect the flocks from the wolf and the lion, whose very appearance in the poem underlines just how little concerned Blake is with describing the realities of the English countryside he knew so well. The two beasts do not actually inhabit the same regions of the earth. They are here yoked together, nevertheless, as symbols of unspecified ferocity and danger. Already we feel the Tyger stalking in the wings.

Of Blake's two treatments of unhappy love in this collection, the song "My silks and fine array," is the more obviously derivative of Elizabethan lyric in its vocabulary and phraseology - though here, too, something fresh and autonomous has been created. But it remains a simple dirge. The enigmatic "How sweet I roamed from field to field" is more ambitious (interestingly, both are observed by women).

> How sweet I roam'd from field to field,
>   And tasted all the summer's pride,
> 'Till I the prince of love beheld,
>   Who in the sunny beams did glide!
>
> He shew'd me lilies for my hair,
>   And blushing roses for my brow;
> He led me through his gardens fair,
>   Where all his golden pleasues grow.

With sweet May dews my wings were wet,
  And Phoebus fir'd my vocal rage;
He caught me in his silken net,
  And shut me in his golden cage.

He loves to sit and hear me sing,
  Then laughing, sports and plays with me;
Then stretches out my golden wing,
  And mocks my loss of liberty.

The language is that of pure 17th century lyric, and individual lines recall poets as different as George Herbert and Andrew Marvell. But the psychology is that of a later century. In its rueful exploration of the tyranny implicit in the love contract between the sexes, it prefigures the later - and darker - "Eternity" and "The Clod and the Pebble" .

These are some of the poems which make up the lyric portion of *Poetical Sketches*. They give a foretaste of what Blake was to achieve not so very long afterwards in *The Songs of Innocence*. But not all the work in the collection is at this level. Blake's imitations of Spenser indicate clearly enough that he was better at innovating than copying. His unfinished verse drama *King Edward the Third* reads like a work of extreme youth. The blank verse is only fitfully successful and the fragment has no dramatic power. The ballads "Fair Eleanor" and "Gwin, King of Norway" are plainly derivative of contemporary exercises in the form.

A more serious question mark is to be placed against the extended prose poems of *Poetical Sketches*. If Blake's early lyrics prefigure his later mastery of the form, these largely shapeless ramblings might perhaps set up a sense of unease about what would happen if Blake were to abandon the lyric stanza for the epic prose poem. "Samson" is intelligible (if not enjoyable) because we are familiar with the biblical story. "Then She Bore Pale Desire" (not printed with the *Poetical Sketches* but, like them, composed before 1777) is not. Too many abstract ideas, too many moral concepts are personified at once. Mere rhetoric is not enough to weld them into a coherent whole. And Blake's sense of rhythm, so assured in the short lyrics, totally deserts him.

3 SOCIETY AND MARRIAGE

Blake stayed with Basire for seven years, completing his apprenticeship at the age of 21. His next period of study, at the newly founded Royal Academy, was to be a less congenial and certainly less profitable experience. At that period the Academy was presided over by the septuagenarian George Michael Moser, a venerable artist of the decorative school, and, like Henry Fuseli (Johann Heinrich Füssli) who was later to find Blake "a good man to steal from", Swiss. The ethos of the Academy, with its emphasis on drawing from life, was one from which Blake could get little. He had already firmly decided which were to be his guiding principles in art. When Moser good-naturedly suggested to him that he might benefit from browsing among the pictures of Rubens and Charles Lebrun, Blake took one look, and indignantly dismissed the advice. The fact that the exuberant genius of Rubens and the insipid flatteries of Versailles court painter Lebrun were of a vastly different order, and should not have been mentioned in the same breath, was not what irked him. The mere notion of such principles qualifying for the description "art" threw him into a rage. We do not know what Moser's reaction was to Blake's expostulation: "These things that you call finished are not even begun: How then can they be finished?"

But more distinguished men than Moser were to feel the brunt of the young student's obstinate contempt. When the President of the Royal Academy himself counselled him to paint with "less extravagance", Blake not only had had no ears for his advice but was indignant for long afterwards that it should ever have been given (although he had sought the great man's opinion in the first place). He was later to dismiss Reynolds in the baneful sentence: "This Man was Hired to Depress Art". Blake's total intolerance of the opinions of others, unhesitatingly expressed face to face, is undoubtedly one of the root causes of his later isolation. It does not of course invalidate the invigorating torrent of opinion which courses through his later *Annotations to Sir Joshua Reynolds's Discourses* and constitutes a prophetic attack on the Academy's adherence to rigid canons of taste.

But the Royal Academy experience was not an entirely negative one. A man in his early twenties - and one furthermore not long afterwards to be married - had to be thinking in terms of an income. Whatever else he did not get from it, the institution introduced him to other artists who could later be useful to him, among them Fuseli, Flaxman and Stothard. Henry Fuseli, whose own eccentric genius (although pronounced "Shockingly mad" by the tepid Gothic fantasist Horace Walpole) managed to find some acceptance by the public, respected his qualities to the end of his life. And although he generously acknowledged theft from Blake, there are instances in which it is clear that Blake returned the compliment. The figures of the scorning friends on the right of Illustration X of Blake's *Job* bear a striking resemblance to Fuseli's much earlier sketch *The Three Witches*. Both men shared a preoccupation with Milton, as their respective versions of *Satan, Sin and Death* clearly indicate. Blake thought that Fuseli's *Satan building the Bridge over Chaos* was one of "the grandest efforts of imaginative art". In many ways the two men were congenial spirits. Both painted from the imagination and had no time for the natural world. Fuseli's pretence of having to put up an umbrella in front of a Constable landscape, to protect himself against such slavish imitation of nature was a gesture which would have been dear to Blake's heart.

Blake acknowledged their friendship in a quatrain in which his robust affection walks well ahead of his poetic talents;

> The only Man that e'er I knew
> Who did not make me almost spew
> Was Fuseli: he was both Turk & Jew -
> And so, dear Christian Friends, how do you do?

But, though early in their lives there was some congruency of interests, it could never have led to a real affinity of ideas. Fuseli, essentially, inhabited the world of the surreal. His forte was terror, nightmare and suspense. He did not live on Blake's spiritual plane. But he always acknowledged his old fellow student's powers. One of the saddest vignettes of Blake's twilight years is his visiting the Academy again and being spotted by Fuseli, by then Keeper, with: "What! You here, *Meesther* Blake? We ought to come and learn of you, not you of us!"

On a more immediate and practical level, his contact with Stothard and through him Flaxman were useful to Blake. Both men were later to feel the force of Blake's biting wit, after various suspicions and misunderstandings that arose out of their association with him. But for now, Stothard, whose charming but somewhat superficial draughtsmanship had already earned him some reputation as a book illustrator, was able to to put some engraving work Blake's way. Flaxman, a sculptor who was by this time becoming known for an output of classical statuettes, also befriended and tried to help him. That his later introduction of the poet to the poetaster Hayley ended in disaster can hardly be held against him. Through Flaxman, Blake met the Rev Henry Mathew and his wife Harriet, who had some reputation as a bluestocking and presided over one of the minor London salons of the day. This introduction gave Blake his first and only experience of belonging to a social and literary milieu.

In the meantime Blake had married. His famous introduction to his future wife is of a piece with an impetuous character which did not know the meaning of dissembling. Blake was lamenting the fickleness of a girl to whom he had been paying court, to Catherine Boucher, the daughter of a Battersea market gardener with whom he was apparently staying. The girl declared that that she pitied him from her heart. "Do you pity me?" Blake enquired, "Then I love you." "I love you, too" came the reply, and the bargain was struck. Only the momentous nature of the exchange redeems this scrap of dialogue from banality and oblivion. Blake's ingenuous nature was to lead him into errors in the judgement of human character on many occasions thereafter. But he was right in the forming of the one crucial relationship. Literally "on the rebound", in a highly vulnerable, not to say self-pitying, frame of mind of a sort in which sensible decisions about a future partner are almost never made, he picked one of the few women on earth who could possibly have made a companion to his genius. True to that first

15

impulse, he was to love her until the day he died.

They were married on 18th August, 1782, in Battersea Church, which had been completely rebuilt not long before, in 1777. Gilchrist somewhat dismissively describes it as "a whitey- brown brick building in the church warden style, relying for architectural effect, externally on a nondescript steeple, a low slate roof, double rows of circular-headed windows and an elevated western portico". Today's Londoners, who have seen so much of their riparian architectural heritage obliterated, are, by contrast, surprised and delighted afresh to come across this reticent neoclassical curio peeping out from behind a giant, derelict flour mill, its churchyard washed by the tidal Thames.

Catherine signed the register with an X, an indication that she was illiterate. But, if she could not write, she was certainly not inarticulate in a general sense. In a later letter to Flaxman's wife (the sculptor had married in 1781) she expresses herself with polish and imagination. It took, it seems, a very few years for Blake to convert a girl who was barely educated, from the conventional point of view, into someone who could give him a good deal of help with his work, copying his verses, drawing and colouring his engravings.

They were never to have children, and over the nature of their sexual relations there is an almost impenetrable veil. Clearly Catherine was no prude, or she could never have consented to be surprised with him by a visitor sitting in their summerhouse listening to *Paradise Lost*, "freed from 'those troublesome disguises' which have prevailed since the Fall", as Gilchrist has so definitively described it. But we do not know what she thought of his invocations to free love in the prophetic books: "lovely copulation, bliss on bliss", of his theories that wives ought to be held in common, or of the sexually explicit marginalia that adorn some of his manuscripts.

In spite of his roamings on the wilder shores of sexual possibility, there is no biographical evidence that Blake was ever unfaithful to his wife, or that he ever wanted to be, much less that he ever seriously contemplated the expansive sexual menage of an Eric Gill. We may have a description of wifely jealousy in the poem "My Pretty Rose

Tree" in the *Songs of Experience,*.

> A flower was offer'd to me,
> Such a flower as May never bore;
> But I said "I've a Pretty Rose-tree,"
> And I passed the sweet flower o'er.
>
> Then I went to my Pretty Rose-tree,
> To tend her by day and by night;
> But my Rose turned away with jealousy,
> And her thorns were my only delight.

But the evidence is purely internal. There is no record of Blake's refusing the advances of another woman and of Catherine's failing to be grateful for his constancy. There is the occasional eruption of dissatisfaction confided to the pages of the 1793 notebook:

> In a wife I would desire
> What in whores is always found –
> The lineaments of Gratified desire.

But Blake is hardly unique in having thus mused. Perhaps, like so many men before and after him, he would also have had to ask himself: But would a whore listen to me reading Milton, or help me with my engraving? His references to Catherine in his letters are always those of a man to whom his wife is a partner in his life's work. When she is ill, he is quick to retail his concern to whomever it is he is corresponding with. Occasionally the steady devotion flashes into something more like passionate admiration, as when, for example, in a latter to Hayley, he describes Catherine as being "like a flame of many colours and precious jewels". A sketch of his wife done at roughly this period shows her to be certainly no beauty. A rather full, solid face is dominated by a more than generous endowment of nose. Language of this enthusiasm tends to confirm that Blake's attachment was, as one would expect in a man like him, to her inner qualities. Although sex and its place in the scheme of things was a constant preoccupation with him, he was not a man with a conventionally roving eye.

An in some ways similar author, James Joyce, offers a parallel. Although fundamentally preoccupied with sex (the arts of which he had learnt from prostitutes) and the creator, in Molly Bloom, of one of the most compelling promiscuous women in world literature, Joyce does not, after his marriage to Nora, appear to have strayed much. If Richard Ellman's assertion that the encounter with Marthe Fleischmann was not truly a sexual one seems to be in some doubt, given the opportunities afforded Joyce by the greater libertarianism of the Continental ethos in which he lived, it hardly amounts to womanising. Both Blake and Joyce were extravagantly gifted men married to "ordinary" women. (They had, also, made the proposals that were to affect their future after a remarkably short acquaintance.) Both evidently valued what they had, and confined their sexual wanderings to the imagination.

Liberal enough in most of his notions, James Blake seems not to have approved of the humble station of his son's bride. The newly-weds did not live with him, as Blake had been doing, but set up home in rented lodgings not far away, near what is now Leicester Square. Sir Joshua Reynolds had a splendid house on the square itself.

From this period early in their marriage dates Blake's introduction into the Mathew menage by Flaxman. The sculptor had been taken up by the pair at an early age and had, in gratitude, executed a number of statuettes for the drawing room of their elegant house in Rathbone Place. This was the meeting place for a culturally and socially conscious society which was characteristic of its day: refined, yet reasonably open-minded; fashionable, yet capable of philanthropy. These qualities were epitomised in the person of Elizabeth Montagu, a woman at once formidably cultivated and energetically philanthropic. She had gained renown some years before for writing an essay on Shakespeare, which Dr Johnson had dismissed as "pack-thread". She had gained her revenge by going to war with him over his essay on Lord Lyttleton in his *Lives of the English Poets,* which had appeared in 1779. Her philanthropy took the form of a famous annual May Day dinner for chimney sweeps.

Harriet Mathew had a no doubt sincere desire to 'help on' struggling artists and poets. It was an honest impulse that led her to persuade her husband to share with Flaxman the cost of having Blake's *Poetical Sketches* printed, although the fact that the copies were never properly published or offered for sale largely vitiated the value of gesture for the author. Mathew's insufferably patronising preface to the edition – going, as it did, well beyond the customary modest disavowal of merit – cannot have helped:

> The following sketches were the production of an untutored youth, commenced in his twelfth and occasionally resumed by the author until his twentieth year; since which time, his talents having been wholly directed towards the attainment of excellence in his profession, he has been deprived of the leisure requisite to such a revisal of these sheets, as might have rendered them less unfit to meet the public eye.
> Conscious of the irregularities and defects to be found in almost every page, his friends have still believed that they possessed a poetic originality, which merited some respite from oblivion.

Blake was not a man to bring any artistic production to birth on such conditional terms.

If as an author he was to be damned with such faint praise, as a society lapdog he did not fare much better. At first he had a certain curiosity value. He not only recited his poems but could sing them, too, apparently to airs of his own spontaneous composing. He knew nothing of music, but his melodies were apparently good enough for established musicologists in the company to try to note them down.

But a man of Blake's convictions and his uncompromising manner of expressing them could hardly be comfortable for long with such a society, nor it with him. For with all its liberal notions a club like that of the Mathews modelled itself on the dictates which Reynolds was to codify in his *Discourses* . The artist who, like Blake, was without formal education was to be "curious and docile" in the company of the "learned and ingenious men" with which the age abounded. He was to treat them with the "respect and deference which is so justly their due", in the hope eventually of acquiring "a rational and systematic taste imperceptibly formed". Alas, these august arbiters of taste could not know that Blake was no empiricist. He could not even begin to believe that his mind could be improved by their polite discourse. "Man Brings All that he has or can have into the World with him", he was later to say. His Neoplatonism envisaged the soul as moving effortlessly between eternity and time. He entered the Mathews' well-meaning drawing room already armed with the wisdom of immortality. He came not to learn, but to instruct.

Blake's pugnacious exposition of his opinions, his intolerance of what he considered wrong-headed, were too indigestible to the palate of the Mathews' salon. There was no particular explosion to end the association. It died of its own accord. After a certain point no one wanted to hear any more of his fiery enthusiasm for topics they could not understand.

His verdict on the Rathbone Place phase of his life is recorded by Blake in a curious satirical work, scribbled down as a series of short chapters in a notebook sometime in the mid-1780s and only, long after his death, published as *An Island in the Moon.* Its interest is not only biographical, although Blake himself makes an appearance, caricatured as Quid the Cynic, and other members of the Mathew circle are readily identifiable.

An Island in the Moon is something of a rag bag, perhaps not surprisingly, since it was only intended as a private jotting, a letting off of steam. But in parts it shows Blake to be quite at home in a literary mode he was never afterwards to pursue. In its mixture of colloquial prose dialogue and, often crude, short verses it shows an ear for the vernacular which is at a far remove from the sonorities of the later works. As the assembled philosophers become more disordered in their thinking Blake whips up an atmosphere of scatological frenzy that puts us in mind of James Joyce's later celebrated excursion into Nighttown.

"I say, this evening we'll all get drunk - I say - dash! an Anthem, an Anthem!" said Suction.

Lo the Bat with Leathern Wing,
Winking & Blinking,
Winking & Blinking,
Winking & Blinking,
Like Doctor Johnson.

Quid. "Oho", said Dr Johnson
To Scipio Africanus,
"If you don't own me a Philosopher,
I'll kick your Roman Anus"

Suction. "Aha", to DrJohnson
Said Scipio Africanus,
"Lift up my Roman Petticoat
And kiss my Roman Anus"

And the Cellar goes down with a step. (Grand Chorus)

"Ho, Ho, Ho, Ho, Ho, Ho, Ho, Hooooo, my poooooor siiides! I should die if I was
to live here!" said Scopprell. "Ho, Ho, Ho, Ho, Ho!"

What possessed Blake in the final chapter of *An Island in the Moon*
suddenly to still this rising tempest of nonsense and let drop the first
poignant notes of the *Songs of Innocence* is impossible to imagine.
Certainly it defies all artistic logic. The scene is "Another merry meeting at the house of Steelyard the Lawgiver" (identified as Flaxman).
Inflammable Gas (Joseph Priestley, the discoverer of oxygen) has
been "pumped quite dry". Mr Obtuse Angle (Thomas Taylor, mathe-
matician, philosopher and religious commentator) is asked for a song.
Instead of the quibbling doggerel he has already given us in a previous chapter, he delivers to the company instead:

Upon a Holy Thursday, their innocent faces clean,
The children walking two & two in grey & blue & green,
Grey headed beadles walk'd before with wands as white as snow,
Till into the high dome of Paul's they like Thames' waters flow.

O what a multitude they seem'd, these flowers of London town!
Seated in companies, they sit with radiance all their own.
The hum of multitudes were there, but multitudes of lambs,
Thousands of little girls & boys, raising their innocent hands.

Then like a mighty wind they raise to heav'n the voice of song,
Or like harmonious thunderings the seats of heaven among
 Beneath them sit the rev'rend men, the guardians of the poor;
Then cherish pity lest you drive an angel from your door.

This is the first draft of "Holy Thursday", which we shall later meet
in the *Songs of Innocence*. When Mr Obtuse Angle has finished we are
told: "After this they all sat silent for a quarter of an hour". Clearly,

21

Blake has exhausted his vein of satirical indignation and is thinking ahead. More ribaldry is called for, but *An Island in the Moon* never returns to its previous vein of scurrility. Further drafts of *Songs of Innocence* make their appearance.

Finally (and here, frustratingly, a leaf of the manuscript is missing) we come in on the end of what is clearly a discussion, being conducted within Blake's mind. Most of it is lost, but we hear Quid saying "I would have all the writing Engraved instead of Printed". After his fruitless experience with conventional letterpress in the production of the *Poetical Sketches*, Blake has come to a decision. From now on, through the technique of etching on copper plates and colouring the results by hand, he will become his own publisher.

4 INNOCENCE AND EXPERIENCE

The five years between 1789 to 1794 separate the appearance of the *Songs of Innocence* and the *Songs of Experience.* In that period Blake produced much else: four of the prophetic books, *The Book of Thel, The French Revolution, The Visions of the daughters of Albion* and *America,* besides that remarkable play of fancy and concentrated wit, *The Marriage of Heaven and Hell.* Nevertheless, when *the Songs of Experience* make their debut in 1794, it is in harness with the earlier engraved book as *The Songs of Innocence and Experience,* with the sub-heading *Shewing the Two Contrary States of the Human Soul.* No copy of the *Songs of Experience* etched as a separate work exists.

In this slender double collection is distilled a perhaps unexampled exploration of the states that exist between unquestioning spiritual idealism and the tainted life of the flesh, deeply experienced. There are artless lyrics born of the belief that humanity, unsullied by what it has done to enslave itself, is without sin. There is incandescent rage against social injustice as Blake saw it everywhere around him. There are poems of sorrow and compassion for what children have to endure at the hands of their parents and of the lawfully-constituted authority of Church and State. There are disturbing glimpses into the unswept corners of the human psyche. And finally there are poems which appear to ask God himself what his purposes for the creation really are. It is utterly remarkable that Blake does so much in the compass of little more than two score short poems.

There are pairs of lyrics in the *Songs,* which by their very titles invite direct comparison. Both collections have their Nurse's Songs, Chimney Sweepers and Holy Thursdays. Other poems, of similar title, appear not to be precise contrasts, while a third category, which contains "The Lamb"/"The Tyger", "The Blossom"/"The Sick Rose", is clearly intended to provide some sort of thesis and antithesis. Yet others of the poems in each collection stand by themselves without an obvious counterpart. Blake is here, anyway, very much poet first and seer/preacher (as he later too often became) second, and it is a mistake to look for too close a cor.

Onto the innocent vision of
Island in the Moon, Blake pours ...
grim realities of existence for the

> Is this a holy thing to see
> In a rich and fruitful land,
> Babes reduc'd to misery,
> Fed with cold and usurous hand?
>
> Is that trembling cry a song?
> Can it be a song of joy?
> And so many children poor?
> It is a land of poverty!
>
> And their sun does never shine,
> And their fields bleak & bare,
> And their ways are fill'd with thorns:
> It is eternal winter there.
>
> For where-e'er the sun does shine,
> And where-e'er the rain does fall,
> Babe can never hunger there,
> Nor poverty the mind appall.

The final stanza gives a glimpse of a world where these things might not be so, but the glimpse remains in the sphere of the optative rather than the actual. The reality conveyed by the poem, in the pitiless repetition of "And their.....", is of a present poverty and neglect which appals the mind, and not of some far-off place where hunger might be assuaged. The bleak exterior world of the poem is warmed only by Blake's burning indignation.

Here, society is at fault. In the two poems entitled "The Chimney Sweeper" it is the mercenary cruelty of parents that comes under attack. Even in the *Innocence* poem the version of the events of the little sweep's life to date is related with shocking baldness:

> When my mother died I was very young,
> And my father sold me while yet my tongue
> Could scarcely cry 'weep! 'weep! 'weep! 'weep!
> So your chimneys I sweep, and in soot I sleep.

But Blake vouchsafes to the sweeps an angelic vision which has the

...em more tolerable to them (not entirely
...s the one poem of innocence from which an
...t cannot be completely banished). Its   corollary
...on contains not even that shred of comfort.

...lack thing among the snow,
...ng 'weep! 'weep! in notes of woe!
Where are thy father and mother? Say?"
"They are both gone up to the church to pray.

"Because I was happy upon the heath,
And smil'd among the winter's snow,
They clothed me in the clothes of death,
And taught me to sing notes of woe.

"And because I am happy & dance and sing
They think they have done me no injury,
And are gone to praise God & Priest & King,
Who make up a heaven of our misery."

By this time the merely uncaring parents of the *Innocence* poem
have become creatures of positive malevolence towards their child.
And Blake's indignation has become a white hot rage that threatens
the coherence of his message. Without knowing in advance that the
line "And because I am happy and dance and sing" refers to the May
Day dance of chimney sweeps, we might not be able to comprehend
how the little boy can have even moments of happiness, given the catalogue of suffering he describes. In the sweeping dismissal of the final
line God, the Church and the monarchy are indicted along with the
parents for their acquiescence in a social order that can create such
conditions. In the potent shorthand of Blake's anger, what should have
been sources of love and care are seen as agents of a monstrous
tyranny.

In "Infant Joy" and its corollary "Infant Sorrow" we advance
beyond social criticism to a consideration of the state of being, itself.
The former is a spontaneous outpouring on the blessing of life, as the
poet contemplates a new-born infant.

Pretty joy!
Sweet joy but two days old,

Sweet joy I call thee:
Thou dost smile,
I sing the while,
Sweet joy befall thee!

The reverse side of this beatific vision could scarcely be more stark:

My mother groan'd! my father wept.
Into the dangerous world I leapt:
Helpless, naked, piping loud:
Like a fiend hid in a cloud.

Joy has fled. The child has entered the world only through the pain of his mother's labour. His father, far from rejoicing in an heir, already fears a rival. It is now a "dangerous world" that awaits him. An equivocal element has, too, entered the equation of being. The child himself appears uncertain as to how beneficent an act his creation really is: "Like a fiend hid in a cloud" recalls the "Mad Song" of the *Poetical Sketches*. And the notion "Shades of the prison house begin to close/Upon the growing boy", later articulated by Wordsworth, is anticipated in the second of the poem's two stanzas, and expressed with concentrated force:

Struggling in my father's hands,
Striving against my swadling bands,
Bound and weary I thought best
To sulk upon my mother's breast.

From the very first, the parental caresses and blandishments are seen in terms of prison bonds, and the intimate, life-giving physical relationship between the suckling mother and her infant is turned on its head as being a source of permanent resentment.

This capacity to concentrate large areas of experience into short lyric lines is one of Blake's greatest strengths. It is never more powerfully demonstrated than it is in the *Songs of Experience*. "The Sick Rose" is perhaps the most striking example.

O Rose thou art sick!
The invisible worm
That flies in the night,
In the howling storm,

26

Has found out thy bed
Of crimson joy:
And his dark secret love
Does thy life destroy.

The two quatrains present the reader with a series of images which suggest conflict taking place on a number of different levels. The flower of the garden has been invaded by a loathsome maggot which is desecrating its heart; a woman has been possessed by a man in a way that diminishes her and destroys her dignity; in more general terms, woman's capacity for love is polluted by some malevolent influence which knows how to prey on it and corrupt it; cosmic and divine love themselves are under attack from a baneful force which inhabits a universe of outer darkness. The worm, whether we think of it as the maggot which attends the putrefaction of organic matter, the invasive penis, or as the serpent which first brought evil into the world, is rendered doubly menacing by Blake through the strange qualities he attributes to it: its invisibility, its capacity to fly, its inhabiting the night and the howling storm. And the poem is given added resonance by the implication that the Rose, in keeping to itself a "bed of crimson joy" in the first place (one which has been "found out" like some guilty secret), has committed the sin of possessiveness which has contributed to its own destruction.

This wealth of suggestions is contained in a poem which is, its opening injunction apart, a single, urgent sentence.

A similar concentration of images is achieved in what is perhaps Blake's best-known poem and one of the most famous short poems in the English language "The Tyger".

In acknowledgement of the school of critics which holds that, in Blake, illustration and text are indivisible and should not be considered separately, it is perhaps best to confront the graphics of "The Tyger" first. In the illustrations to the various etched versions of "The Sick Rose" Blake concentrated on the phallic aspects of the worm, which is seen emerging from the heart of the bloom, crawling up the thorny stems and apparently ravishing various female forms in the process. This reduction of the poem to a purely sexual statement is in itself a limitation. Nevertheless it clearly depicts one of the identifiable themes of the poem, and the illustrations have an undeniably repellent fascination.

But what are we to make of the amiable quadruped which props up the bottom of the plate of "The Tyger"? Is it, as in David Erdman's theory, "one of Blake's contrived enigmas - a contrivance forced upon him by the truth"? (Whatever that may mean.) Does it have something to say to us about a reconciliation between the Tyger and the Lamb which the poem certainly leaves unresolved? Or is it simply a failure in the artist's sense of what is visually appropriate here? The image is so totally lacking in the symbolic charge of the words that the last conclusion seems to me inescapable.

Tyger! Tyger! burning bright
In the forests of the night,
What immortal hand or eye
Could frame thy fearful symmetry?

In what distant deeps or skies
Burnt the fire of thine eyes?
On what wings dare he aspire?
What the hand dare sieze the fire?

And what shoulder & what art,
Could twist the sinews of they heart?
And when thy heart began to beat
What dread hand? & what dread feet?

What the hammer? What the chain?
In what furnace was thy brain?
What the anvil? what dread grasp
Dare its deadly terrors clasp?

When the stars threw down their spears,
And watered heaven with their tears,
Did he smile his work to see?
Did he who made the Lamb make thee?

Tyger! Tyger! burning bright
In the forests of the night,
What immortal hand or eye
Dare frame thy fearful symmetry?

It is possible to limit the host of possibilities set up in this poem, by referring to Blake's symbolic system. In this scheme of things the stars become reason, the agents of Urizen (the line is later echoed in *The Four Zoas* where the subservience of the stars to Urizen is made explicit). By the same token, in his reference back to the Lamb of the *Songs of Innocence*, Blake appears to want us to see the Tyger as a direct antithesis. Thus, the Tyger becomes Blake's evil, authoritarian Jehovah/Urizen figure in opposition to the Christ of his Lamb, who is beneficent, creative and is, for Blake, the one true God.

I think it is a pity, as well as being a mistake, to systematise a reaction to the poem along these lines. For a start, "The Tyger" works and always has worked for those who have never troubled themselves with Blake's mythology and symbols. And the poem, after all, states nothing positive. It takes the form of a series of questions which are not even rhetorical ones. "Did he who made the Lamb make thee?" remains deliberately unanswered at the end.

The fact is that the impact the Tyger makes on the imagination is not that of the Urizenic force which Blake so abhorred. Rather he appears as one of the Tygers of Wrath, those beings of imaginative energy so dear to Blake. He is a splendid creature, but one which seems to bear little resemblance to the terrestrial carnivore *Panthera tigris*, much less to the docile tabby cat of Blake's illustration. He has been brought to birth in some cosmic furnace by a smith endowed with even more terrific powers than himself. But though he is continually described in terms such as 'fearful', 'dread' and 'deadly', he is, as a spectacle, undeniably exhilarating.

In *The Songs of Innocence* Blake ended "The Lamb" with the line "Little Lamb, God bless thee!" In the *The Marriage of Heaven and Hell* he gives us the provocative aphorism "Damn braces: Bless relaxes". The Tyger falls undoubtedly into the first category. His power is more likely to be purgative than destructive. T. S. Eliot is surely, consciously or unconsciously, echoing him in "Gerontion" in the lines "In the juvescence of the year/Came Christ the tiger". The paradox is one with which Blake would have been thoroughly at home.

In *The Marriage of Heaven and Hell* Blake floats the idea "He who desires but acts not, breeds pestilence". In *Songs of Experience* he graphically explores the damage done by emotional repression in "A Poison Tree".

I was angry with my friend
I told my wrath, my wrath did end.
I was angry with my foe,
I told it not, my wrath did grow.

And I water'd it in fears,
Night & Morning with my tears
And I sunned it with smiles,
And with soft deceitful wiles.

And it grew both day & night'
Till it bore an apple bright
And my foe beheld it shine
And he knew that it was mine.

And into my garden stole,
When the night had veiled the pole
In the morning glad I see
My foe outstretched beneath the tree.

The technique here is markedly different from that of "The Sick Rose" where the emotional charge seemed to propel and mould the verse itself. Here, there is total control, creating an atmosphere of deadly calm. The repetitions of 'I' and 'And' at the beginning of lines lend it an atmosphere of artless, ballad-like, simplicity which is ironically at odds with the seething emotions being monitored. Blake is such a master of these effects that it is a puzzle to find the touch deserting him in the longer poems. The echoes of Eden and the inversion of the idea of the Tree of Life only serve to reinforce the irony.

These, then, are some of the characteristic strengths of the *Songs of Innocence and Experience*. Psychologically and sociologically speaking, they are as revolutionary as they are spiritually daring. They anticipate by five years that later and more conscious revolution, in which two poets, after careful consideration, set out to "make the incidents of common life interesting by tracing in them, truly though not ostentatiously, the primary laws of our nature", as Wordsworth was to describe his and Coleridge's intentions in the *Lyrical Ballads*.

We have only to read the *Lyrical Ballads* by the side of the *Songs of Experience* to appreciate the more comprehensive nature of Blake's achievement. By comparison with Wordsworth and Coleridge he sounds modern. They find themselves compelled to go to "low and rustic life" for the human material with which to achieve their effects. And the language in which they write is often self-conscious in its avoidance of 'poetic' effects. Yet the "youthful harlot's curse" which Blake hears on London's midnight streets, which doubles up as the syphilis with which she will inflict her, as yet unborn, children, would have been subject matter as unthinkable to them as it would have been unacceptable to the audience they were trying to educate in their new way of seeing things.

The modest reforms of the *Lyrical Ballads,* although they required several strenuous prefaces from Wordsworth to elucidate them, nevertheless made a reputation for their authors. Blake's collections fell on deaf ears. It was not until several generations later that poetry was to be able to handle the subjects he did with such unforced candour and psychological truth.

5 THE LAMBETH YEARS

In 1790 Blake and his wife moved south of the river, to Lambeth. It was to be the beginning of a happy and productive period for Blake. It was one, too, in which he enjoyed moderate prosperity. Among the works of this period are the politically-conscious prophetic books: *The French Revolution* (1791) and *America* (1793), the sexually-emancipated *Visions of the Daughters of Albion* (1793) and the prose masterpiece, *The Marriage of Heaven and Hell.*

But these really have their genesis in the period which immediately preceded the move. After leaving the polite society of the Mathew circle Blake had become associated with a company whose ideas were much more congenial to him. It was a time of international political ferment and upheaval. Most liberal opinion in England had been on the side of the American colonists in their struggle for independence. Until Terror darkened the scene it was, likewise, for the French revolutionaries. For Wordsworth "Bliss was it in that dawn to be alive". For Blake it meant a wholehearted engagement with the tenets of the Friends of Liberty, who watched events in France and wondered whether a similar transition from autocracy to republic could be effected bloodlessly of course in England.

Chief among such spirits was the publisher Joseph Johnson who had been one of Blake's main employers for engraving work ever since his Royal Academy days. At his house gathered a circle which included at various times the apostle of the American revolution Thomas Paine and Joseph Priestley, who in addition to having discovered oxygen was one of the principal apologists for the French Revolution. Also among visitors to the Johnson house were the social reformers William Godwin and Mary Wollstonecraft (later to become Godwin's wife and, posthumously, the mother-in-law of Shelley).

How intimate Blake was with this circle is open to question. He was not, in any case, a 'circle' man and would have had no difficulty falling out, even with like minds, over some detail of an opinion whose precise formulation did not appeal to him. But he shared its general ideas, was an enthusiast for the revolution in France and (until the advent of the Terror, at least) sported its symbolical red cap. Mary Wollstonecraft's brave pioneering work *A Vindication of the Rights of Woman* predates his *Visions of the Daughters of Albion* by two years.

Man acutely conscious of social injustice Blake was not of a character to confine his protests solely to his verse. He was a pugnacious opponent of wrong wherever he saw it taking place. There are several stories from these years of his personally intervening to prevent a young boy from being maltreated by his employer or a wife from being abused by her husband.

Blake was short and stocky, with something of the bulldog about him. Most drawings and sketches of him emphasise his corporeal solidity quite as much as they do his inner spirituality. The long walks he had taken from earliest childhood and continued after his marriage kept him physically fit. When roused, he was a formidable opponent, as an irate dragoon, later famously to be frogmarched from his garden and hustled unceremoniously for fifty yards down the road, was to discover.

Blake had annotated Swedenborg's *Wisdom of Angels concerning Divine Love and Divine Wisdom* and his *Wisdom of Angels concerning Divine Providence* in 1788 and 1790 respectively. In the process he had, as he so often did with those he was at first disposed to admire, increasingly fallen out of love with the tenets of the master. The repeated seal of approval, "Mark this" of the earlier commentary has become "Cursed Folly!" before the end of the second, as Blake takes issue with Swedenborg's ideas on predestination.

In his own *The Marriage of Heaven and Hell*, etched not long after the second of the series of annotations, Blake develops his own ideas in a series of aphorisms and sketches which are pregnant with thought and rich in paradox. They encapsulate his readings from the Gnostics and dilate on the errors of Swedenborg, whose writings are dismissed by the end as being merely "a recapitulation of all superficial opinions". But *The Marriage of Heaven and Hell* can be read and savoured without reference to either the Gnostics or Swedenborg. It is

Blake's most felicitous performance as a pure thinker. Notions at once provocative and irresistible in the truth they distill are dispensed in a prose that seems to revel in itself.

The poetic introduction which purports to state the argument is the weakest part of the book.

Rintrah roars & shakes his fires in the burden'd air;
Hungry clouds swag on the deep.

Once meek, and in a perilous path,
The just man kept his course
Along the vale of death.

It is when Blake abandons mythology for aphorism that *The Marriage* comes into its own. The famous critique of Milton's *Paradise Lost*: "The reason Milton wrote in fetters when he wrote of Angels & God, and at liberty when he wrote of Devils & Hell, is because he was a true Poet and of the Devil's party without knowing it", has a permanent place in the corpus of Milton commentary. In "A memorable Fancy" Blake relates with assured impertinence:

As I was walking among the fires of hell, delighted with the enjoyments of Genius, which to Angels look like torment and insanity, I collected some of their Proverbs; thinking that as the sayings used in a nation mark its character, so the Proverbs of Hell show the nature of Infernal wisdom better than any description of buildings or garments.

After this iconoclastic provocation Blake proceeds to a series of paradoxes which constitute a concentration of wisdom unequalled, perhaps, anywhere else in English prose. Scarcely one of the "Proverbs of Hell" is redundant. Blake treats us to a torrent of ideas any single one of which might make a volume from the pen of any other author. Thus "The road of excess leads to the palace of wisdom" could be regarded as the philosophical basis of much of the output of D. H. Lawrence. "Eternity is in love with the productions of time" is an idea frequently recurred to and worked out in the novels of E. M. Forster. "If the fool would persist in his folly, he would become wise" distils a dimension of Russian culture which finds its most memorable expression in Dostoyevsky's *The Idiot*.

"The cistern contains, the fountain overflows", "One thought fills immensity", "The soul of sweet delight can never be defiled" are typically exuberant Blakean assertions. A nugget of wisdom of a completely different sort is: "He who has suffer'd you to impose upon him, knows you." Just occasionally we are brought up short. An age which has seen both national and individual criminality on the scale ours has may feel the need to think twice about "Sooner murder an infant in its cradle than nurse unacted desires". But Blake is not legislating for the pathological personality here. The proverb merely carries to the limits the statement "He who desires but acts not, needs pestilence", the implications of which are worked out in "The Poison Tree". Rintrah just anger against the restrictions with which Urizen continually tries to constrain the mental universe is at the back of many of the *Proverbs*. The "tygers of wrath" are invoked to release us from our tendency to enslave ourselves with proscribed opinion. Blake is here in a mood to exult in the richness and variety of the physical and spiritual creation. In four swift and vivid assertions he reminds us:

> The pride of the peacock is the glory of God.
> The lust of the goat is the bounty of God.
> The wrath of the lion is the wisdom of God.
> The nakedness of woman is the work of God.

This sums up Blake's assurance of the holiness of living things. For all the mental mountaineering that goes into the later prophetic books, he was never really to surpass it.

Blake had begun to compose in the free verse style of the later prophetic books as far back as *Tiriel* which he seems to have written about the same time as the *Songs of Innocence*. It has no obvious thematic link with the rest of the prophetic books. It opens with Tiriel, king of the "western plains", being rejected by his sons who are resentful of his past misdeeds. There are clear echoes of *King Lear*, both literally: "Serpents not sons" , "Bless thy poor eyes, old man", and in the general theme of the piece. But there is little else to remind us of Shakespeare. *Tiriel* is a rambling performance whose nerveless verse:

> He wander'd day & night: to him both day & night were dark.
> The sun he felt, but the bright moon was now a useless globe:
> O'er mountains & thro' vales of woe the blind & aged man
> Wander'd, till he that leadeth all led him to the vales of Har.

betrays a certain infirmity of purpose in its author. Perhaps Blake sensed this since he did not etch it or attempt to get it published.

The Book of Thel, which immediately follows it clearly foreshadows the sexual preoccupations which Blake was to make explicit in Visions of the Daughters of Albion. Thel, a virgin shepherdess lives in the "vales of Har" a sort of otherworldly utopia where, with her sisters, she tends her sheep. But she is dissatisfied and has intimations of an existence outside this framework. As she wanders about she is greeted by, successively, a lily, a cloud, a worm and a clod of clay, who indicate to her that her life can be a more significant thing if she engages the real world. But when, at the invitation of the clay, she enters this "land unknown" she is terrified by the sight of her own "grave plot" and by a battery of rhetorical questions from a "voice of sorrow". Unable to face these new possibilities she shrinks from the experience. Blake suggests that she is a pre-existent spirit, who must enter the world to put on mortality, a notion derived from his study of Greek thought at that time.

The plates which illustrate the poem suggest a more specifically sexual dimension to Thel's desires and fears than the text does. Apart from its final lines:

> The virgin started from her seat, and with a shriek
> Fled unhindered until she came into the vales of Har.

the debate to which Thel is subjected is largely philosophical. But in the title page she gazes wisfully into the middle distance, where a naked youth flies through the air and greets a young woman, gowned like Thel is, with a passionate embrace. The following plates reinforce the emphasis on a sexual theme. In Plate 4 the cloud to which she has just finished speaking is personified by yet another barely draped young man whose rapturous course across the sky seems to preoccupy Thel far more than the worm to whom she should be listening.

36

In Plate 5 a voluminously attired Thel sits moodily over the "matron clay" and the worm, who are personified as a nude woman and her child, and is clearly unable to share their naked intimacy. The final plate, a naked girl and two infants riding on the back of a serpent, makes an ironic gesture in the direction of sex and the Fall, at the same time implying (through the manifestly untroubled exuberance of the children) that neither sex nor the Fall will be as terrible to Thel as she fears.

Yet in spite of the fact that its themes are clear enough, there is something provisional about *Thel* as a poem. The neoplatonism of its final section may have been a later addition by Blake. The verse itself lacks impact. The blank verse heptameters (which are not always perfectly sustained by Blake) engender a sense of ennui.

In the *Visions of the Daughters of Albion* this tentativeness is dispelled. There are certain elements of the background to this poem which may help to the understanding of it, but they are not essential. The protagonist Oothoon is derived from Ossian's Oithona, the virgin of the waves. Blake's perception of the "soft soul of America" reflects his belief in the purity of the new nation across the Atlantic, in marked contrast to a Europe compromised by centuries of *Realpolitik*. References to the "swarthy children of the sun" derive from Blake's experience of illustrating, for Johnson, the harrowing *Narrative of a Five Years' Expedition against the Revolted Negroes of Surinam* by a retired soldier John Stedman. Published in 1796, Stedman's account of the cruelties inflicted on the slaves included, to his eternal credit, the admission that he had himself been "married" for five years to a young black slave whom he had later abandoned to her fate after she had borne him a child .

Engraving such subject matter at a time when the debate on slavery was at its height in England, focused Blake's anger against the iniquities of colonialism. His compassion for opppressed races and for women is expressed in engravings for the Stedman *Narrative* which are as different as the charming *Europe supported by America and Africa*, in which a black, a white and an American Indian girl lovingly embrace, and the brutal *A Negro hung alive by the Ribs to a Gallows*, a shocking image in which Blake's sense of outrage is, nevertheless, firmly under the control of his deep, silent pity.

The dramatic situation of *Visions:* is simple enough. Oothoon, a virgin, is seen at the outset wandering disconsolately "Along the vales of Leutha", a place apparently synonymous with only 'officially sanctified' sexual relations. She plucks a marigold and is filled with the desire to fly to Theotormon and consummate their love. On the way she is intercepted by the authoritarian Bromion (Greek ßpomios: roaring) who rapes her, impregnating her at the same time. Unfortunately for her Theotormon agrees with Bromion's estimate of this act of violence, i.e. that it constitutes a defilement of her and that she is now "Bromion's harlot". (So, astonishingly does Frye, who quaintly described her rape as "an extramarital amour".) Theotormon gives way to jealousy from which Oothoon spends the rest of the book trying to dissuade him. At first she does so in terms which are apologetic, even calling "Theotormon's eagles" (in a clear reference to the punishment of Prometheus for stealing fire from the gods) to "rend away this defiled bosom". As his intransigence continues (at her mutilation by the eagle he "severely smiles") her apologetic tone becomes progressively merely conciliatory:

> "Silent I hover all the night, and all day could be silent,
> If Theotormon once would turn his loved eyes upon me;
> How can I be defiled when I reflect thy image pure?"

and, then, as he reveals himself to be as hidebound in his sexual attitudes as Bromion, positively defiant. Finally she breaks into a paean in praise of sexual love.

> And does my Theotormon seek this hypocrite modesty,
> This knowing, artful, secret, fearful, cautious, trembling hypocrite?
> Then is Oothoon a whore indeed, and all the virgin joys
> Of life are harlots, and Theotormon's is a sick man's dream,
> And Oothoon is the crafty slave of selfish holiness.
>
> But Oothoon is not so, a virgin fill'd with virgin fantasies,
> Open to joy and to delight wherever beauty appears.
> If in the morning sun I find it, there my eyes are fixed

In happy copulation; if in evening mild wearied with work,
Sit on a bank and draw the pleasures of this freeborn joy"

This is an innovatory sexual manifesto by the standards of 18th-century literature. And there is more to come from Oothoon. Without having to suffer further interruption from Theotormon, who has by now withdrawn completely into himself, she lets her rapture continue into realms which make it a revolutionary enough tract for any age.

"I cry, Love! Love! Love! Happy, happy love, free as the mountain wind!
Can that be Love that drinks another as a sponge drinks water?
That clouds with jealousy his nights, with weepings all the day:
To spin a web of age around him, grey and hoary, dark!
Till his eyes sicken at the fruit that hangs before his sight.
Such is the self-love that envies all! a creeping skeleton
With lamplike eyes watching around the frozen marriage bed.

But silken nets and traps of admanant will Oothoon spread
And catch for thee girls of mild silver, or of furious gold:
I'll lie beside thee on a bank and view their wanton play
In lovely copulation bliss on bliss with Theotormon...."

The illustrations have the same sensuous and sensual vigour as the text. On the first page, which retails the argument, we see a naked Oothoon clasping the marigold to her breast while she kisses the young child which represents its human personification. At the head of the plate entitled "Visions", which describes her defilement by Bromion, a series of tiny naked figures wantons in the skies. Two males are shooting Cupid's bows while a young girl rides astride a gigantic, squat penis as if it were a horse, its *glans* rearing between her thighs. At the foot of the page lie Oothoon and Bromion, mutually, it would seem, exhausted after the violence of their sexual encounter. This picture is slightly ambiguous and may represent Theotormon's view of them as an "adulterate pair", since Oothoon's clothes appear to be lying by her, flung off as if in careless rapture, rather than being torn and still hanging in tatters on her, as would be more likely in a violent rape.

In the next plate we see her lying on her back, thighs spread wide, while the eagle comes to claim its share of her flesh. There is ambiguity here, too. Utterly prostrate though Oothoon is, she is lying in an undeniably sexually inviting posture, "writhing her soft, snowy limbs" as the poem puts it. There is more than a suggestion of sexual awakening here, and that the "eagle" of the text, which in the illustration completely lacks that bird's hooked beak, may be analogous to the Zeus/swan which visits Leda for sexual purposes.

There is a marvellous economy in these drawings which are some of the best on the small scale that Blake ever achieved. In a later plate the utter misery of Theotormon and Oothoon is graphically depicted as, naked, they hang wretchedly about in each other's presence, seemingly unable to tear themselves away, but equally unable to embrace. Although Blake adheres to the convention of not depicting male and female genitalia, these illustrations carry a compelling sexual charge. Blake is here completely in control of his artistic medium.

The ending of the poem is inconclusive. There is to be no reconciliation. The daughters of Albion, Englishwomen enslaved by sexual custom as Oothoon is, can only sigh and sympathise. But the interest of *Visions of the Daughters of Albion* is rather in its emancipated content than in its success as a poem. Simply, Blake deals here with the question of relations between the sexes in a manner which anticipates Freud and the 20th century.

6 REVOLUTION AND PROPHECY

Between *Thel* and *The Visions of the Daughters of Albion* stands *The French Revolution*, Blake's first attempt at history, composed in 1791. A number of critics, Frye, Erdman and Ackroyd among them, have seen this as one of his most important poems, not merely because of its intrinsic merits (though they estimate those highly) but because Blake's failure to publish it was crucial to his later development. The loss of the opportunity to publish it, they maintain, robbed Blake of an audience and consequently of a critical sounding board. It drove him increasingly into himself, leading him to the determination to engrave and thus "publish" his works himself.

But this argument cannot be divorced from the question of the poem's merits. If Johnson, whom Blake calls the publisher on his title page, had issued the poem and it had been a failure, it seems unlikely that Blake would have profited, creatively speaking, from the experience. And as we have already seen, Blake had made the decision to engrave his work after the debacle of the *Poetical Sketches,* to ensure its transmission to his audience in the form he wanted it. We do not know why *The French Revolution* was not published. It contains no detectable seditious matter of a kind that might have inhibited Johnson. Blake has left us no clues as to why it never appeared, nor why the last six of the seven books he promises us on the title page were never, apparently, written.

The one extant book has been much admired. For Frye it is "a fine and durable poem". To Erdman, in it Blake "came closer than he ever would again to making his interpretation of history comprehensible to the English public of his own day". Even the generally more temperate Mona Wilson detects "tremendous voices....above the tumult of Ossianic metaphor". But in her very praise she has identified the poem's principal drawback. It is a heavily rhetorical *fortissimo* performance which deals in a strangely static manner with the momentous events it describes.

King Louis XVI and his nobles are in council:

As in day of havock and routed battle, among thick shades of discontent,
On the soul skirting mountains of sorrow, cold waving the Nobles fold round the King;
Each stern visage lock'd up as with strong bands of iron, each strong limb bound down as with marble,
In flames of red wrath burning, bound in astonishment a quarter of an hour.

It is heavy going. Blake's customary ability to startle with images fails him. The juxtapositions: stern visages and iron, and binding of limbs with marble cry out for transposition. For once, the surprise effects of which Blake is so capable do not work; for once there seems to be no reason not to to have done the 'obvious'. The pedestrian detail of "a quarter of an hour" brings the whole description bathetically to earth. One only has to place it beside the magnificence of Milton's council of fallen angels, with which it begs comparison, to be painfully aware of the magnitude of Blake's failure here. Had *The French Revolution* been released on the public it is difficult to imagine what it would have made of it.

When Blake returned to history in *America* (1793), it was to produce something of a very different sort. *America* is as much mythological as historical. The plodding narrative form of *The French Revolution* has been jettisoned for something which more wholeheartedly exists in the realms of the imagination. There is a reference to the main events of the American War of Independence. The King of England, Washington, Franklin and Paine all make their appearance. But this is a war which takes place as much in heaven as in the pages of history. Some of the symbols of Blake's cosmogony as he eventually evolved it are already in place: Orc, spiritual revolt; Urizen, repression; and Albion, the troubled soul of England. We also encounter a maid-like figure who has many affinities with Oothoon.

In their style and subject matter the illustrations to *America* both refer back to and advance from those of *The Visions of the Daughters of Albion*. Thus, the "soft soul of America" is ravished by the horrors of war, in an illustration which is a clear echo of Oothoon's "punishment" by the eagle, though on this occasion the bird most certainly is the bird of prey, armed with hooked beak and talons, and appears actually to be rending some flesh from the prostrate female form. Most of the plates are in fact dominated by the graphics. Some contain only a few, fugitive lines of text, which are jostled by the energetic forms that cavort madly within the space allocated to them.

The poem's mood of exaltation is summed up in the invocation to freedom on Plate 6, which is surmounted by a naked seated youth who gazes skywards.

> The morning comes, the night decays, the watchmen leave their stations;
> The grave is burst, the spices shed, the linen wrapped up;
> The bones of death, the cov'ring clay, the sinews shrunk and dry'd
> Reviving shake, inspiring move, breathing, awakening,
> Spring like redeemed captives when their bonds & bars are burst.
> Let the slave grinding at the mill run out into the field,
> Let him look up into the heavens & laugh in the bright air;
> Let the inchained soul, shut up in darkness and in sighing,
> Whose face has never seen a smile in thirty weary years,
> Rise and look out......

The rapturous tone and to a certain extent the vocabulary recall irresistably the *Song of Songs*.

In the whole series of long poems we loosely term the prophetic books, this is the first of only two which are actually subtitled "a prophecy" by Blake. The second is *Europe*, which is dated the following year. But by that time the bright optimism with which Blake and his fellow radicals had greeted the French Revolution was becoming difficult to sustain. Revolution had turned to Terror, and from Terror it was to evolve into a tyranny (in the purely Greek sense of the word) with imperial ambitions that did not seem so different from those Blake had deplored in the government of England.

The later Lambeth Books do not strike out onto the tides of history with that same ringing confidence of tone. In *The First Book of Urizen*, *The Song of Los*, *The Book of Ahania* and *The Book of Los*, which take us up towards the end of the period of Blake's Lambeth domicile, the preoccupation is with the evolution of the personal mythology. The long, flowing lines which characterised the books from *Thel* onwards, have become truncated. There is a constipated, inward-looking quality in verses like these from *The First Book of Urizen*:

Ages on ages roll'd over him;
In stony sleep ages roll'd over him,
Like a dark waste stretching, chang'able,
By earthquakes riv'n, belching sullen fires :
On ages roll'd ages in ghastly
Sick torment; around him in whirlwinds
Of Darkness the eternal Prophet howl'd,
Beating still on his rivets of iron,
Pouring sodor of iron; dividing
The horrible night into watches.

It is difficult to imagine that the sheer monotony of these piled epithets can have proceeded from the same inspiration that produced the *Songs of Experience.* Never would Blake on his top poetic form, so to speak, have allowed the repetition of "ages roll'd" to carry so scant a charge, or to achieve so little poetic effect. Yet the *Urizen* lines are close, in point of time, to those of the *Songs* and *Visions.* They cannot be the product of an inspiration which has begun to suffer from the lack of an audience to provide it with a shaping discipline. They are, rather, the product of an imagination in thrall to the message.

The lines describe Urizen himself, a symbolic figure fundamentally important to Blake's metaphysical thinking. Urizen is the Jehovah of the Bible as Blake sees him, the creator of the world but also a tyrant who circumscribes man's thoughts and actions. In later books he is opposed by Los, an imaginative principle, who, with his female "emanation" Enitharmon (who stands for a range of qualities, spiritual beauty and inspiration, though these are capable of being corrupted), gives birth to Orc, a spirit of revolution. Together they battle to assail Urizen in his mental and moral fortress, which has been built in the mills of logic. It is these, and not the mills of the industrial revolution (which Blake would never have encountered), that are the "dark Satanic Mills" made so famous by the poem "And did those feet in ancient time......"

This is an inevitably simplified summary of the preoccupations which Blake works out in *The Book of Urizen, The Song of Los, The*

44

Book of Ahania and *The Book of Los* and which bring him to the threshold of the last and most massive of the Lambeth Books, *Vala, or the Four Zoas*. The problem with the books is that they are concerned with problems i.e. the working out of Blake's philosophical ideas to the detriment of the poetry in which they are written. If they are read closely their arguments can be followed, but without a very great deal of pleasure. They come perilously close to being turgid to the point of vitiating an interest in their content.

This is reflected in the illustrations to these books which inhabit a lower plane of inspiration than those of the group which precedes them. The swooping figures of the *Visions of the Daughters of Albion* and *America* recalled Tintoretto in their zestful defiance of the forces of gravity. Here the draughtsmanship is leaden, the modelling static and heavy, the pulse of inspiration faint. Even granted the fact that the themes are sterner, we feel that Blake, like his Urizen, has become entrapped in the cocoon of his ideas in a manner whch has momentarily destroyed his power to embody his concepts in visual form. There is an almost tangible sense of immense labour for results which we grudgingly acknowledge rather than deeply feel.

Vala or *The Four Zoas* was the last of the books Blake began at Lambeth. He began it in 1797 and worked on it for up to perhaps ten years after that. But it was never published, and remained a manuscript until this century. The fact suggests that he eventually had another poem in view more fully to express the themes he explored in it. *The Four Zoas* began as a series of jottings on the proofs of Young's *Night Thoughts* which Blake had been commissioned to illustrate. The nine nights of Blake's poem were probably suggested by the similar structure of Young's.

A complete exegesis of the poem's four thousand-odd lines is impossible here. Most of its symbolic principals have already been encountered. The four Zoas aspects of the mental, spiritual and physical creation are Urthona/Los, representing the imagination; Luvah/Orc, wrath and passion; Urizen, reason and control; and Tharmas, physical man and his compassion. They have their respective female emanations: Enitharmon, Vala, Ahania and Enion. In a series of conflicts these various aspects of the human soul work out the poem's theme: the Fall, the creation of universal man and, hence, the nature of the spiritual universe.

The result is over-complex. The fact that several drafts exist of some of its parts does not help us in deciding what exactly Blake intended as a finished product. But the principal themes are clear enough. Above all, Los and Enitharmon, the forces of spontaneity and imagination, are perpetually at war with the authoritarian Urizen.

The poem is too long, working and re-working its themes in exhaustive detail which becomes in itself exhausting to the reader. But it has sustained passages of beauty and passion which recall the energy of the earlier Lambeth books. The lament of Enion, compassionate emanation of Tharmas:

> "Why does the Raven cry aloud and no eye pities her?
> Why fall the Sparrow & the Robin in the foodless winter?
> Faint, shivering, they sit on leafless bush or frozen stone
> Wearied with seeking food across the snowy waste, the little
> Heart cold, and the little tongue consum'd that once in thoughtless joy
> Gave songs of gratitude to waving cornfields round their nest."

recalls similar evocative complaints from Oothoon as she ponders her sexual rejection by the man she loves. Later on in the poem we see Los and Enitharmon, Blake's indefatigable champions of man's and woman's humanity:

> Descending sweet upon the wind among soft harps & voices
> To plant divisions in the soul of Urizen & Ahania,
> To conduct the voice of Enion to Ahania's midnight pillow.
>
> Urizen saw & envied....

Urizen, jealous at the very thought that his consort Ahania may become imbued with the imaginative instincts enjoyed by Los and Enitharmon, strongly recalls Milton's Satan, filled with envy as he spies on the innocent embraces of Adam and Eve in the Garden of Eden (a subject Blake was later to illustrate with great effect).

The Four Zoas ends with a Last Judgement. At the outset of Night the Ninth we learn:

as a prelude to the final apotheosis:

..........The war of swords departed now,
The dark Religions are departed & sweet Science reigns.

It is not, however, to be Blake's last word on the subject.

The sexual marginalia to *The Four Zoas* are fascinating and cannot be ignored. They are not merely sexually explicit, but in the range of the sexual activity they depict: masturbation by both men and women, defaecatory and group sex, buggery, fellatio, etc, have seemed to some to be unusual excrescences of the mind of a man who is in the poem engaged in the mightiest of spiritual struggles.

Perhaps some of them are in the nature of doodles, and need not be taken too seriously. After all Blake had not prepared this MS for formal publication. And yet, for Blake sex *is* a cosmic and not merely an earthly problem. The notion, "The nakedness of woman is the work of God", is for him a profound truth. Sex, as we know it, is for Blake a division of the oneness of the human spirit, which must somehow be reconciled. He exalted the sexual act as no Christian had done before him. It is that which gives rise to his deep loathing of sexual relations and acts that degrade (as they so often seem designed to do) the female. "They [most men] take it for granted that Woman's Love is Sin; in consequence all the Loves & Graces with them are Sin" he had said as early as the *Annotations to Lavater* (c1788). It is against this background that the sexual imaginings of Oothoon are to be judged in the *Visions of the Daughters of Albion.* Woman is degraded by man's desire to possess her in secrecy, in a manner conforming to his own code. The theme surfaces in *The Four Zoas.* Urizen, as usual the culprit:

Builded a temple in the image of the human heart
And in the inner part of the Temple, wondrous workmanship,
They formed the Secret place, reversing all the order of delight,
That whosoever enter'd into the temple might not behold
The hidden wonders allegoric of the Generations
Of secret lust, when hid in chambers dark the nightly harlot

47

Plays in Disguise in whisper'd hymn & mumbling prayer. The priests
He ordain'd & Priestesses, cloth'd in disguises beastial,
Inspiring secrecy.....

This is may not be great, nor even good, poetry. In his loathing of
male manipulativeness Blake is in danger of drowning in the turbu-
lent waters of his own rhetoric. But the message is clear: the authori-
tative Urizen has turned the whole world of spiritual and sexual
delight on its head. Hymns are whispered and prayers are mumbled.
Whatever might have been beautiful has become beastly. Whatever
should have been open has become secret and disguised.

In one of the marginal drawings to *The Four Zoas* Blake represents
a woman's genitalia as a Gothic church porch. No interpretation of it
can redeem it from being a bizarre, even ludicrous, image. But given
the groundswell of Blake's indignation against the desecration of
woman within the poem itself, it can, perhaps, be seen as something
more than a moment of idle erotic fantasy.

We saw above that *The Four Zoas* began life on the proof sheets of
an edition of Young's *Night Thoughts* . Commissioned by the book-
seller Richard Edwards, it was to have been a de luxe edition of a
poem which had enjoyed immense popularity with 18th-century read-
ers from the appearance of its first volume in 1742 onwards. (It is now
chiefly remembered for the single line: "Procrastination is the thief of
time".) This was a potentially lucrative commission for Blake, with
several hundred illustrations called for. And, though the subject matter of Young's tedious philosophisings cannot much have interested
him, it presented Blake with new technical challenges. Advancing a
stage from what he had achieved in his own work images surround-
ing the text each page of verse would now be placed in, and be subor-
dinate to, the graphic that illustrated it.

Alas for Blake, a project that might have ensured him a degree of
freedom from want ended in commercial disaster. Renewed war with
France was drying up the sources of artistic patronage. Like other pro-
jects of its type (Fuseli's Milton Gallery was one of them) the venture
had to be aborted. Only one of the projected four volumes was ever

published, and that used far fewer than the 156 designs Blake had done for it.

And yet, these last years of the 18th century were ones crowded with visual, as they were with poetic, creativity for Blake. Ironically, while he was increasing the complexity of his verbal output, he was refining a style for his paintings and prints which took them away from the constraints of representational realism (of which he was always somewhat impatient) into the sphere of pure emblem. The single year 1795 gives us some of his most memorable images: the colour prints *Elohim Creating Adam, Satan Exulting Over Eve, Newton* and *Nebuchadnezzar.* In these and other pictures of this period, it is as if Blake, freed at last from the shackles of space and perspective that had dominated European painting since the Renaissance, can communicate direct to us the vision inwardly perceived by him. Yet, in spite of their otherworldly power, these pictures are as unlike the nightmarish visions of Fuseli or the overwrought visual melodramas of John Martin as can be imagined. Like Blake's simplest poems, they come before us almost as things that have existed since the beginning.

In 1799 Blake had the second stroke of luck in a life which was not to be noted for its happy encounters. What possessed Thomas Butts, a lowly official in the office of of the Commissary General of Musters, to become the artist's patron on quite the terms he did, is a mystery. Commissions apart, Butts simply took what Blake produced over the next twenty years and paid him a small but regular wage for it. And when he commissioned works for himself, he did not interfere, as many of Blake's patrons did, with the artist's treatment of the subject. "Fifty small Pictures at One Guinea each" (as the biblical subjects of 1799-1800 were) were life blood to Blake and gave him an artistic satisfaction that copying or engraving other men's work could not. Whatever else his shortcomings, for standing as he did "between the greatest designer in England and the workhouse", as Samuel Palmer put it, Butts deserves, a niche of honour in the history of art.

7 THE FELPHAM DISASTER

In 1800 Blake and his wife moved from London to Felpham in Sussex. There for the next three years he worked as an engraver and illustrator for William Hayley, poet, essayist and country gentleman. The introduction had been made in a well-meaning spirit by Flaxman who felt it would offer Blake a steady income. Because of Hayley's status (he was a landed proprietor and friend of Gibbon and Romney) and known powers of patronage, it might also present Blake with the means permanently to better himself.

In the event, although the association took Blake from London for only three years, it was, for him, a profoundly disastrous one. There were external circumstances which helped to bring matters to this conclusion. Mrs Blake's health suffered severely from the sea winds and the damp of a country cottage whose tenants could not afford to heat it properly. Because of an altercation with a soldier in his garden Blake found himself on trial for sedition, a circumstance which caused him a great deal of anxiety and undoubtedly took a toll of his creative energies. But the main cause of the trouble was the relations between Blake's new patron and his dogmatic employee.

Much critical bile has been expended on Hayley who was certainly complacent and shallow as well as being a versifier of such negligible talents that the name poet dignifies them absurdly. Undoubtedly he patronised Blake insufferably, was oleaginously insincere and tried to 'reform' his tastes and improve him in a dozen other little ways which would in any circumstances have become exasperating to a man of Blake's temperament.

Yet none of this ought to have discomposed Blake as much as it did. It might have been good for a spiteful verse aside, but he certainly should not have let it invade the inner sanctuary of his mind, the place he kept holy for the reception of higher truths. He had met plenty of shallow, insincere people before and had had to put up with hack employment to turn a shilling. The fact is that he let Hayley anger him to such a degree that it threatened to compromise his artistic integrity.

For a man even of such violent antipathies and enthusiasms as Blake, some of the pronouncements spawned from the Felpham years suggest a loss of sense of proportion. He accused Hayley of attempting to seduce his wife; he accused him of trying to frame him over the sedition charge; he taxed him with being a "spiritual enemy"; he abused him behind his back in verse and in prose. Most seriously, he let a man who should never have been allowed a status greater than that of an irritant even if a severe one come to personify a fundamental evil in one of his most ambitious symbolic works. It is this which mars *Milton*, in which at moments Satan appears, in the qualities attributed to him, closely to represent all that Blake deprecated in a man like Hayley. It hardly needs saying that a merely stupid, self-regarding Sussex country squire should never have been allowed to symbolise a towering spiritual concept like Satan, in what was intended as a major epic poem.

Given the sad end to the Felpham adventure it is almost pathetic to read the high hopes with which Blake embarked on it. To Flaxman he rhapsodises in a letter of 12th september 1800:

> My Dearest Friend,
> It is to you I owe All my present Happiness. It is to you I owe perhaps the Principal Happiness of my life..........

While to a letter to Hayley himself written shortly afterwards he appends the optimistic postscript:

> My fingers emit sparks of fire with expectation of my future labours.

Alas, tasks like those Hayley had in mind for him at Felpham were not of a sort to likely to strike any sparks from Blake. Not only was the material he gave Blake to illustrate imaginatively impoverished, but having given him a commission he would practically stand over his designer and insist that his own notions of decorum were complied with.

One has only to glance at the engravings for Hayley's *Ballads*, to see what a backward step they represent for Blake in terms of his graphic and inspirational development. The subject matter is wretched stuff. The full title was *Ballads, by William Hayley, Esq, Founded on Anecdotes relating to Animals, with Prints, Designed and Engraved by William Blake.* The quality of theme Hayley proposes to handle is indicated by "The Dog", a poem which tells the wholesome tale of a pet who, to prevent his young master from swimming in crocodile-infested waters, hurls himself in first. He is snapped up by one of the waiting reptiles, bringing the wilful youth to his senses. Nevertheless this act of self-sacrifice shows the canine to be, indeed, man's best friend.

Blake does his best with this drivel. But the fact of his having to employ a solemn Augustan style of representation only underpins the threadbare nature of the subject matter. Blake can seldom have had to stoop so low as he does in an illustration which shows the small terrier plunging from a cliff into the gaping jaws of a ludicrous cayman whose natural home would seem to be the Punch and Judy show. Not satisfied with dragging Blake's genius in chains behind his squirely chariot, Hayley compounded the offence by observing in a patronising preface to the first edition of the *Ballads*: that he had written them to provide "such literary relaxation as might relieve my own mind, and still more amuse a friendly fellow-labourer, whose serious occupation gives him a better claim to such indulgence: I mean my friend, Mr Blake, the Artist".

Blake's reaction to this fantastic piece of self-delusion is not on record. But we do know that he subsequently used spare sheets of the *Ballads* (which were originally issued separately) as scrap paper. It does, in fact, seem to have taken a little time for it to sink in to Blake just how utterly incompatible his new patron was likely to prove. And his later comment "Corporeal friends are spiritual enemies" is one of the few of his aphorisms in which exasperation far outweighs wisdom. Blake's tragedy in this situation is that he should ever taken Hayley, at the latter's own estimation, as a friend (rather than merely as a patron) in the first place. It is a canker which gnaws away at the cosmic heart of *Milton* and is responsible for some of that poem's most confusing moments.

But however pernicious Hayley's effect on Blake's creativity, he stood by him during the entire course of an incident which could have had serious consequences for Blake. On a summer's day in 1803 a private from a troop of dragoons locally quartered was encountered by Blake in the garden of his cottage at Felpham. The man seems genuinely to have been under the illusion that he had been invited there to help with some gardening that Blake was having done. Blake did not know this, and asked the man to leave. We have only Blake's word for it that he did so "as politely as possible". One half doubts it, although the evidence suggests frankly that the man may have had a drink or two. (He had previously been reduced from sergeant to private, for drunkenness.) An altercation ensued which ended with Blake forcibly ejecting the soldier from the garden and then pushing him more than fifty yards up the road, the man attempting all the while to turn and get in a blow at his furious assailant. The scene as one envisages it has a ludicrous rather than dramatic quality: Blake a less than five-and-a-half foot bundle of fury, hustling an impotent warrior of the king's Life Guards in front of him, firmly pinned by the elbows.

The sequel was not so comic for Blake. Once inside his quarters, the local Fox Inn, Scofield (or Scolfield, there are two extant versions of the life guardsman's name) decided, after getting together with a fellow soldier, to lay a treason charge before local magistrates on the grounds that Blake had uttered seditious thoughts against his King, the government of his country and against (a cunning afterthought in a rural area with a strong sense of local pride) the good sense of the English people. The text of the alleged expressions is famous, but is worth giving again. Blake, it was alleged:

> did utter the following seditious expressions, viz., that we (meaning the people of England) were like a Parcel of Children that would play with themselves until they got scalded and burnt, that the French Knew our Strength very well, and if Bonaparte should come he would be Master of Europe in an Hour's Time, that England might depend on it that when he set his Foot on English ground that every Englishman would have his choice whether to have his Throat cut or to join the French, and that he was a strong man and would certainly begin to cut Throats, and the strongest Man must conquer - that he damned the King of

England - his country and his subjects, and that his soldiers were all bound for Slaves, and that all the Poor People in General - that his Wife then came up, and said to him, this is nothing to you at present, but that the King of England would run himself so far into the Fire that he might get himself out again, and altho' she she was but a woman, she would fight as long as she had a drop of blood in her - to which the said - Blake said, My Dear you would not fight against France - she replyed no, I would for Bonaparte as long as I am able..."

Scofield certainly deserves some marks for creative effort. The above has a certain breathless quality about it which is almost plausible. And it is a nice touch to bring Mrs Blake in. Scofield must have done his homework and knew of Catherine's supportive reputation. The moment of misunderstanding between husband and wife over exactly whose side she is on has, too, a ring of truth about it.

Which brings us to the question of whether Blake could possibly have uttered the words ascribed to him. Most commentators have laughed the suggestion out of court: the diminutive Blake could hardly have had breath to utter such a lengthy tirade while hustling a burly life guardsman in front of him. But Scofield's deposition makes it clear that the alleged words were uttered in the garden, before Blake had begun to expel him. And there is nothing in the alleged tirade that Blake would not thoroughly have concurred with a few years earlier. Blake's best defence is his own reaction to the charges. As a letter to Butts shows, he was thoroughly alarmed by the whole affair. A man of his patent honesty could hardly have failed to let slip some small admission of hotheadedness, had there been any.

The episode may of course have been an attempt to frame Blake because of his known history of radicalism. But that seems unlikely. Blake's sympathy with the French Revolution had been a thing of ten years and more before. A cautious man like Hayley would hardly have employed a man who was perceptibly still seething with Jacobin opinions. That the high treason charge should have ever come to court, given that there was not a witness to substantiate it, seems perhaps absurd now.

But, as Talleyrand was famously to remark: "Le trahison, c'est une question de la date". What might have gone unnoticed in earlier years of radical fervour had become a different matter. The fragile peace of Amiens had just collapsed. The country was in a state of war psychosis and 'Boney' was synonymous with the Devil in English eyes (even on the Continent an ardent worshipper like Beethoven was, not long afterwards, to tear out the dedicatory page of his Bomaparte Symphony and rename it simply *Eroica*). In a part of the country on which an invasion would necessarily have fallen with the most imme-diate force, feelings were running particularly high.

A time of wretched suspense followed for Blake. And yet it had its positive side. Hayley's support of him enabled the rift that was clearly impending between the two men to be smoothed over. Returning to London, Blake kept in touch with his protector (among other things Hayley had put up most of the bail for him) in letters that were neces-sarily friendly, even affectionate. It ought, perhaps, to have been a les-son to Blake that certain types of friendship can operate on a practical level without having, necessarily, to be spiritual ones. But perhaps by then too much bad blood had flowed between the two men. Hayley had not apparently redeemed himself sufficiently to be spared making his Satanic appearance in *Milton*. Nevertheless, when Blake was acquitted of treason at Chichester Quarter Sessions in February 1804 he was sincerely grateful to his erstwhile despised patron.

The Scofield episode is a curious one, psychologically speaking. It is apparently an open-and-shut case. The court and all that literary research has been able to do have acquitted Blake. And yet the biog-rapher always feels the need to rehearse the details afresh. I suspect that we are actually a little disappointed with the result. At a time of war fever, when finer feelings must so often be subordinated to the 'common good' of coarsely-expressed jingoism, our hackles instinc-tively rise against the Scofields of this world. I think we would like Blake to have stood his ground in the manner of which he was accused. Blake pugnaciously behind bars for standing up against that bogus patriotism Johnson called memorably "the last refuge of a scoundrel" would have been an indelible image. Blake frightened of retribution, painfully glad, at last, to be brought to safety through the good offices of a man he so contemned, is something we contemplate with considerably less pleasure.

8 MILTON AND JERUSALEM

After his acquittal Blake was finally able to join his wife permanently in London where, after a short period staying with his brother James, they finally took two rooms in South Molton Street. These cramped quarters were to be their home for the next seventeen years. If Blake had been spiritually unhappy at Felpham, his material condition was to be his bugbear in London. The rest of his life reads like a struggle against neglect and ill usage. If Blake had hopes of coming into regular engraving work he was to be cruelly disappointed. Without Butts's continuing patronage he and his wife must have starved.

Milton and *Jerusalem* are the last two of the major illuminated prophetic books. The latter kept him occupied between 1804 and 1820. One of the extant frontispieces to *Milton* is engraved with the date 1804, although he did not finish the work until 1808. In any event, as we have seen, much of the poem has its genesis in the conflicts of the Felpham years.

Milton is Blake's comprehensive exploration of a theme that had been preoccupying him for years the 'errors' of the author of *Paradise Lost*, and the manner in which they can be reconciled with Blake's general universal scheme. The argument, briefly, runs thus: Milton, who has been walking about in heaven since his death, is in an uneasy frame of mind. He contemplates his "Sixfold Emanation" (his wives and daughters) which is "scattered through the deep in torment". In short, he is unhappy about his own treatment of the female aspect of himself, during his lifetime. He decides to come back into the world, and enters the spirit of Blake. Henceforward the two creative spirits will view their experiences through the same eyes. The result is a conflict with, and the defeat of, Satan, and the reunion of Milton with all the aspects of his female emanation, united now in the person of Ololon.

Opinion is sharply divided about the merits of *Milton*. Its themes are more or less intelligible. The problem comes in the direct comparison Blake's saga of Milton's 're-education' invites with *Paradise Lost* itself. The first book of *Milton* :

> Say first! what mov'd Milton, who walk'd about in Eternity
> One hundred years, pond'ring the intricate mazes of Providence,
> Unhappy tho' in heav'n - he obey'd, he mumur'd not, he was silent
> Viewing his Sixfold Emanation scatter'd thro' the deep
> In torment - To go into the deep her to redeem & himself perish?

deliberately echoes the familiar lines of Paradise Lost:

> ....say first what cause
> Moved our grandparents in that happy state ,
> Favored of Heaven so highly, to fall off
> From their creator and transgress his will
> For one restraint, lords of the world besides?

If Blake's aim is pastiche as a means of rebuking the philosophical direction taken by Milton, then it has to be conceded it is rather a poor one, and, *as poetry,* suffers by comparison with the splendour (as well as with the immediate intelligibility) of the original.

The problem of what one might call aesthetic decorum mounts as *Milton* proceeds. Blake moves with such ease:

> Between South Molton Street & Stratford Place, Calvary's foot,
> Where the victims were preparing for Sacrifice their Cherubim;

that the reader cannot always readily follow. In his grand style Milton strove to create a plausible, if generalised, cosmic scenery against which to stage his spiritual conflicts (and in *Paradise Lost* he never falls so heavily on his face as he does when he descends to specifics such as the digestive tracts of angels). But Blake is, as it were, so much *at ease* in heaven, so assured of the effectiveness of the symbolic personages he has chosen to represent various spiritual states, that he is under no such pressure to make his universe understandable to us.

In addition, the introduction into this process of the conflict between Hayley (Satan) and Blake (as Palambron), with its detail barely digested, is fatal to the integrity of the result:

58

> Then Palambron, reddening like the Moon in an eclipse,
> Spoke, saying: "You know Satan's mildness and his self-imposition,
> Seeming a brother, being a tyrant, even thinking himself a brother
> While he is murdering the just: prophetic I behold
> His future course thro' darkness and despair to eternal death.
> But we must not be tyrants also: he hath assum'd my place
> For one whole day under pretence of pity and love to me.
> My Horses hath he madden'd and my fellow servants injured.
> How should he, he, know the duties of another? O foolish forbearance!
> Would I had told Los all my heart! but patience, O my friends,
> All may be well: silent remain while I call Los and Satan."

This does not work. The association with Blake's grievances against Hayley is too close for the conflict to be universally intelligible. "Mildness" is not a fundamental evil, and "self-imposition" is a short-coming, not a sin. The largeness of the intellectual and moral issues Blake wants to convey is simply not sensed. The language, varying between the colloquial and the weakly high-flown, does no justice to the argument. And in the last two lines there is a descent to the level of frank pantomime dialogue.

Again, we find ourselves puzzling that a man who could have prefaced *Milton* with the exquisite lines:

> And did those feet in ancient time
> Walk upon England's mountains green?
> And was the holy Lamb of God
> On England's pleasant pastures seen?

could not have drawn some benefit from a comparison between them and the peevish rhetoric of Palambron's speech. It seems to me that the oft-repeated assertion that Blake's later obscurities stem from his increasing isolation will not hold water. Here, in a single work, we have Blake writing lyrics as powerful and as charged with meaning as anything in the *Songs of Experience*. Yet, only a few lines later his irritation and dogmatism have got the better of him to the extent that he is incapable of poetry at all.

It may of course be said that we are wrong to judge *Milton* as poetry. That it is the message and not the medium that counts. But Blake was no philosopher (not in the sense that Spinoza, Leibniz and Kant are philosophers). He can certainly *philosophise*, but when he

59

does, it is his habit to do so in striking emblems and aphorisms, in the manner of a poet. His thought is strangled when he enters the jungles of ratiocination. This should not surprise us. When he does, he is doing precisely what he deplored throughout his life in Urizen; he is seeking to impose an order on us. His own inspiration does not survive the attempt.

Milton ends on a note of triumphant assertion. The poet, like Piers the Plowman, awakes from his vision, and:

> Immediately the Lark mounted with a loud trill from Felpham's Vale,
> And the Wild Thyme from Wimbleton's green & impurpled Hills,
> And Los & Enitharmon rose over the Hills of Surrey.
> Their clouds roll over London with a south wind; soft Oothoon
> Pants in the Vales of Lambeth..
> Rintrah & Palambron view the Human Harvest beneath.
> Their Wine-presses & Barns stand open; the Ovens are prepar'd;
> The Waggons ready; terrific Lions & Tygers sport & play.
> All Animals upon the Earth are prepar'd in their strength
> To go forth to the Great Harvest & Vintage of the Nations.

But even the visionary beauty of these lines cannot blind us to the fact that the terrestrial locations: Sussex, Surrey, London SW19 and London SE11 interpose themselves between us and Blake's intended synthesis. They have no place on the cosmic map. Milton, at least, had the wisdom to keep geography out of *Paradise Lost*.

After *Milton*, Blake was to be involved with the composition of *Jerusalem* for much of the rest of his life. Critics who consider it to be Blake's final masterwork, as Bernard Blackstone does, are prone to find that those who prefer *Milton* do so because it is easier, has more accessible passages. In fact *Jerusalem*'s strengths and weaknesses are very much those of *Milton*. But it is not unfair to say that it is more inaccessible for far longer stretches than its predecessor. It is frequently turgid and prosy. The oft-quoted:

> I must Create a System or be enslav'd by another Man's.
> I will not Reason & Compare: my business is to Create.

does not tell us anything about Blake's mental autonomy that we did not know from as far back as *The Marriage of Heaven and Hell*. In its shrill, self-assertiveness it vitiates the very message it intends to convey. And what are we to make of:

> I turn my eyes to the Schools & Universities of Europe
> And there behold the Loom of Locke, whose Woof rages dire,
> Washed by the Water-wheels of Newton: black the cloth
> In heavy wreathes folds over every Nation.........

Blake has, by this time, become an exasperated official from the Education Ministry. The simplistic generalisations do him no justice. We only have to compare them with the controlled anger of:

> But most thro' midnight streets I hear
> How the youthful harlot's curse
> Blasts the newborn Infant's tear'
> And blights with plagues the Marriage hearse.

to feel acutely the loss of imaginative power. In other parts of the poem Blake works out his sense of grievance over his trial for sedition, much as in *Milton* he had vented his irritation against Hayley. At one point even Scofield is held up to us as an object of execration. It goes without saying that a disgraced private of dragoons is not a fit target for Blake's tremendous artillery.

The tendency, noted in *Milton*, for Blake to want to make detailed geographical locations stand for navigational beacons on the cosmic chart reaches almost obsessive proportions in *Jerusalem*.

> Oxford trembled while he spoke, then fainted in the arms
> Of Norwich, Peterborough, Rochester, Chester awful, Worcester,
> Lichfield, St David's, Llandaff, Asaph, Bangor, Sodor,
> Bowing their heads devoted.

It is possible (and we must be grateful to Erdman, Foster Damon and others for making it so) to tease out some sort of specific meaning for each of these references. But that does not help the general reader (even one familiar with the main landmarks of European literature) for whom the poem seems simply to bury itself under a welter of English, European and biblical placenames. In *Jerusalem* it is an even more formidable journey through the convoluted innards of the poem than it was in *Milton* before we can join Blake on the summit of his supreme assertion:

> All Human Forms identified, even Tree, Metal, Earth & Stone: all
> Human Forms identified, living, going forth & returning wearied
> Into the Planetary lives of Years, Months, Days & Hours; reposing,
> And then Awakening into his Bosom in the Life of Immortality.

> And I heard the name of their Emanations: they are named Jerusalem.

Is this "obscure", as Mona Wilson feels, or is it "the vision of the city of God, as focused and clarified by the prism of art" (Frye) And is *Jerusalem* "Difficult not because of sheer incoherence as *The Four Zoas*, but by reason of the complexity of thought, the subtlety of the mental states described, and the interpolation of doctrinal passages which break the narrative." (Blackstone)

The fact is that it is possible to make oneself a Blake 'expert'. The vast field of the prophetic books provides a wealth of opportunity for discussing and deciphering a myriad of symbols at the expense of having to determine either their effectiveness or the intrinsic value of the poems or prophecies to which their existence is germane. We ought not to allow ourselves to be cowed by this process. As is seen in the production of endless books and monographs, it has a self-fuelling tendency.

For the verdict must surely be that, notwithstanding their interest as an index to the mental states to which Blake was often in thrall, the prophetic books cannot possibly repay, as works of art, the colossal effort required to elucidate them. The crux of the matter is: without the *Poetical Sketches*, the *Songs of Innocence and Experience* and *The Marriage of Heaven and Hell* could Blake possibly enjoy his present status? To put it another way: if in the case of Milton we take out of the equation *L'Allegro*, *Il Penseroso*, *Comus*, *Lycidas* and the Sonnets and judge him on *Paradise Lost*, *Paradise Regained* and *Samson Agonistes*, we are still left with a poet of indisputably European stature. A Blake to be judged on the *Four Zoas*, *Milton* and *Jerusalem* alone would almost certainly be no more than a literary curio.

Paradoxically, the illustrations to *Jerusalem* are some of the strongest in any of the illuminated books. In *Milton* the graphics have, by and large, retreated to the margins, as if Blake's concentration on the verbal argument (and *Milton* is perhaps the most purely argumentative of all the prophetic books) has veiled his inner eye. In *Jerusalem* there is a return to a wholehearted marriage of text and graphics, as well as a number of splendid individual plates. Of the latter, Albion contemplating Christ on the Cross has a luminous intensity which has been compared (not totally absurdly) with Grünewald's Isenheim altar *Crucifixion*. And the final apotheosis, Jerusalem, as Man, being enfolded in the arms of Christ the Creator who has at length become reconciled with Jehovah, convincingly expresses the sense of the ultimate union of the human with the divine which Blake so obviously understands, but does not quite achieve, in the poem itself.

9 CREATIVITY IN NEGLECT

The years after the return to London from Felpham were ones of increasing isolation. The financial rewards were few and the recognition scant. Yet the creative faculty, though under siege from what Johnson has so vividly called "that deferred hope that makes the heart sick", never died in Blake. He was to be duped and cheated, as well as insulted, by a mean-spirited man like Cromek over his illustrations to Chaucer and to Blair's poem *The Grave*, but they remain an indelible part of his achievement. There were to be more fine paintings, some commissioned by Butts, others by John Linnell, the young artist who was to be his last patron. Finally, there is his reinterpretation of *The Book of Job*, a work of art which in its mastery of the principles of design and the power of their translation into the graven image is unsurpassed by anything Blake ever did.

If there is anything to be said in mitigation of Hayley in his relationship with Blake, i.e. that he was merely obtuse, vain and patronising rather than actively malevolent, the same cannot be said for Cromek. Robert Hartley Cromek was what these days would be termed a thrusting individual, a man who prided himself on his acuity in business matters. In a glow of no-nonsense self-regard he liked to style himself "engraver, publisher, author and Yorkshireman" After an only moderately successful career as an engraver, he was anxious to launch himself as an entrepreneur in artistic matters. The most dispassionate survey of the evidence suggests that in almost all his dealings with Blake he deliberately set out to deceive him.

In 1804-05 Blake had executed a large number of sketches for Blair's poem *The Grave*, a meditative piece on mortality which had first been published in 1743. Notwithstanding the fact the the *Lyrical Ballads* were now several years old there was still a strong public taste for such things. A few lines indicates its quality:

In grim Array the grisly Spectres rise,
Grin horrible, and obstinately sullen
Pass and repass, hush'd as the foot of Night.

64

Again! the Screech-Owl shrieks: Ungracious Sound!
I'll hear no more, it makes one's Blood run chill.

In a sustained fit of inspiration which soared above this doggerel, Blake created a series of sketches of vigour and originality which are among the best he ever did. Seeing Blake's work and sensing a commercial opportunity, Cromek moved in on the project with a proposal for an edition using engravings of Blake's designs. Blake naturally assumed he was to be the engraver and set to work with enthusiasm. Cromek had other ideas. Judging that for commercial purposes the smooth Italianate style of the popular Luigi Schiavonetti, with whom he had been a student, was a safer proposition than the brooding power of Blake, he engaged the former to engrave the designs. Commercially, he may have been right from a short term point of view. But from a comparison of Blake's and Schiavonetti's rendering of the plate *Death's Door*, it is clear that the timidity of his taste, while lining his pockets, robbed the world of what would have been a series of engravings of dramatic intensity. In its contrast of flickering light with profound interior darkness, Blake's version has the unearthly quality of his Albion contemplating Christ on the Cross. His ancient figure, stumbling into the jaws of the tomb is a King Lear, broken on the rack of life. Schiavonetti's version, bland and tastefully lit, gives us merely an elderly burgher making a decorous progress through a civic doorway.

Blake was naturally angry at the loss of a profitable contract and (so effectively had Cromek manoeuvred) of his copyright. When he tried to recoup something by offering Cromek an illustration for a dedicatory page to Queen Charlotte (for which Blake had obtained the royal permission), he was rebuffed in the most insulting terms. In a letter which has its niche in the annals of insolence, Cromek told him that the dedicatory sketch was superfluous, a matter between Blake and the Queen and nothing to do with him. Yet when the edition eventually appeared in 1806 Cromek was quite happy to use use the dedicatory verses which Blake had forwarded with his sketch, which must have helped sales of the book. Cromek applied further gall by adding gratuitously: "When I first called on you, I found you without reputation; I *imposed* on myself the labour, and an herculean one it has been, to create and establish a reputation for you."

Time has given its verdict on the relative merits of Blake, Schiavonetti and Cromek. But for that moment Blake could only confide in frustration to his notebook:

Cr[omek] loves artists as he loves his Meat.
He loves the Art, but 'tis the Art to Cheat.

What angered Blake even more than this episode was his treatment at the hands of Cromek and Stothard over a project for a painting and engraving of Chaucer's pilgrims. The facts are not completely clear; Stothard may not deserve the share of the blame Blake attributed to him. Blake had begun a sketch of the Canterbury pilgrims shortly after realising he had lost the work for the Blair engravings. Rightly or wrongly, he was under the impression that this intention had Cromek's support. But Stothard was shortly afterwards commissioned by Cromek to begin an oil painting on the same theme. He may have been ignorant that Blake was at work. Cromek certainly did not enlighten him. But certainly he was briefed on the precise details of composition by Cromek, who had seen Blake's sketch. Completing his work while Blake was still in the process of rumination, Stothard had it exhibited in May 1807 amid a very substantial blaze of publicity engineered by Cromek. By the time Blake finished his fresco of the subject almost two years later, Stothard's picture was being exhibited throughout the country by Cromek at the entrance price of a shilling a head, and had become a highly popular engraving.

Blake could only reply with a piece of defiance, touching in its bravery but doomed to failure. In May 1809 he mounted what was to be his last attempt to gain public recognition, an exhibition of sixteen of his pictures in a room above his brother's hosier's shop on the corner of Broad Street. Entrance price was to be one shilling a head. A descriptive catalogue "containing Mr B's Opinions and Determinations on Art, very necessary to be known by Artists and

Connoisseurs of all Ranks" cost two shillings and sixpence (inclusive of the shilling entrance fee).

Pitted against the publicity machine of Cromek this forlorn, shoe-string venture foundered almost without trace. Few came and none bought. Yet the two-and-sixpenny catalogue has its place in the history of literary and art criticism. Burning with rage at what he conceived to be Stothard's treatment of him, Blake vented it in the longest note in the catalogue, that to item No III, *The Canterbury Pilgrims, from Chaucer.*

The result is not only a damning indictment of Stothard's painting. It is, at the same time, a perceptive critique of Chaucer's pilgrims as they are seen in the General Prologue. Blake pointed out to Stothard that the Knight and the Squire should, as Chaucer depicts them, be leading the procession and not, as Stothard has them, be lost in obscu-rity somewhere in the middle of it. He reminded his rival that the Squire is not to be thought of as a fop, but as a gracious, cultivated and chivalrous youth, who "blends literature and the arts with warlike studies". Finally, and with remarkable restraint, given the depth of his indignation, he took issue with Stothard's crass description of the Wife of Bath as "a young, beautiful and blooming damsel" with the dry riposte: "She has had four husbands....." Blake, in short, tried to remonstrate with Stothard, to intimate to him that in entering the world of Chaucer he was not peeping in on some fairground gallery of grotesques, but should have been participating with humility in a moment distilled from our common humanity.

A comparison of the two pictures confirms Blake's instincts. Stothard's, with its ill-digested elements of Rubens and its generally excitable tone, was no doubt congenial to an age whose popular taste was for the flashy handling of Lawrence, Raeburn and Etty. But the processional dignity of Blake's study takes us back to an era and a tra-dition which seem, almost, to predate his beloved Dürer. It has the archaic solemnity of the Master of the Tegernsee Passion's *Crucifixion* in Munich's Alte Pinakothek, or of Simone Martini's *Guidoriccio da Folignano* in the Palazzo Pubblico at Siena.

In these last years, although Blake was occupied with the composition of *Jerusalem*, it is in the productions of his brush and graver that he is at his most memorable. True, he does not produce work of consistent quality. The style, sometimes emblematic, sometimes realistic, sometimes almost surreal, does not always suit the subject. The portraits of kings, ghosts of fleas and other visitants to Blake when he fell into his rapt moods, seem like mere curiosities, and one wonders how much the presence of a gullible enthusiast for such visions like John Varley encouraged Blake in their production.

But he was still capable of images of great beauty and power. Among the best of his paintings are those illustrating Biblical themes, particularly those seen through the intermediary inspiration of Milton: *Satan Arousing the Rebel Angels, Satan Watching the Endearments of Adam and Eve, The Judgement of Adam and Eve, Raphael Warns Adam and Eve* . These, all in the emblematic style, are in striking contrast to his less frequent realistic treatments of similar themes. In Raphael's warning, for example, the figure of Eve has a predominantly hierarchical function as the Mother of Mankind. Her musculature is delineated in much the same terms as that of Adam. Her face serenely but blandly echoes his; her breasts are modelled much as his pectorals are, and are no larger than them. But in the realistic *Eve naming the Birds* she has become an arrestingly pretty and full-bosomed young woman, one whose gaze holds ours with disconcerting directness.

Blake's last two great series of illustrations are those to the *Book of Job* and to Dante's *Divine Comedy*. The latter are well known through the oft-reproduced *Whirlwind of Lovers*. But the Dante illustrations, interesting though they are, do not merit comparison with Blake's *Job*. They are what they purport to be: illustrations to another man's work. Except in small essentials Blake did not have time fully to reconsider an approach to Dante's themes. If he had had, he would surely, for example, have wanted to do something about Dante's approach to sin, which must have been anathema to him.

Job is a different matter. Although Blake had been painting watercolours of various aspects of the Job story since 1805, it is in his own engraved version of the book in 21 plates, done in 1825, that we see what is meant by his 'vision' of the Book of Job. These are not just illustrations of the Bible story. Blake simply could not accept at face value a tale of man's incomprehensible sufferings at the hands of an inscrutable god. His vision is a complete reinterpretation of the story in terms of man's capacity to allow himself to be enslaved by his Urizenic principle, and of the necessity fully to understand and to escape from that condition. In essence, the vision of Job is the last of the prophetic books. But it is a prophetic book in which illustration has, at last, become completely dominant. The text, no longer Blake's but a selection of Biblical quotations marginalised in the surrounds to each illustration, serves merely to nudge us towards an understanding of each engraved stage of the vision. And these engravings are creations of immeasurably greater power than their watercolour prototypes. *Satan Smiting Job with Sore Boils*, is an utterly more evil creation in the vision than he is as the not unhandsome youth of the painting. The reduction to monochrome partly accounts for this. Blake had a capacity to create freakish gleams of light in a way that eluded him in colour. Illustration XI to the Vision, in which Job is haled down to the bottom of the pit under the weight of his own terrified imaginings, oppressed by God and clawed at by demons, is surely one of the most fearsome images Blake ever produced. In its echoes of the earlier painting *Elohim Creating Adam* it suggests an, as yet, unresolved enigma dwelling at the heart of existence.

After the failure of his exhibition of 1809 the glimpses we catch of Blake become less frequent. Fortunate for so many years in the patronage of John Butts, he was to find another good friend in a young painter, John Linnell, to whom he was introduced in 1818. Through him Blake met other young artists, a group who called themselves the Ancients, who looked up to Blake with affectionate respect. Among this group was Samuel Palmer who came to have an unqualified admiration for Blake. Undoubtedly the cheerful friendship of these young, but like, minds, did much to ameliorate these years of near penury.

When Linnell moved to Hampstead in 1824 Blake often visited him there. Blake had, in the meantime, moved to his own last home, Fountain Court, in the Strand. There, though his rooms were by all accounts small and dark, they gave a glimpse of London's river which was so precious to him. His time, now, was almost entirely taken up with etching and engraving.

Although afflicted by a certain number of the complaints incidental to growing old, Blake was able to work with more or less unabated energy up until the last year of his life. But by the spring of 1827 he was becoming increasingly weak and ill. It was not to be a long, slow decline. Although confined to his bed by mid-summer, he was able to write a letter to Linnell on 3rd July. Little more than a month later, on the afternoon of 12th August, he was dead. He had been conscious until shortly before the end, singing joyful songs and assuring his wife of eternity.

10 BLAKE AND HIS TIMES

Blake had died virtually, but not completely, unnoticed. A few short obituaries appeared in the literary periodicals. The jeering tone of the first, in *The Literary Chronicle* on 1st September 1827, set the style for the others:

> The late Mr William Blake, whose recent decease has been publicly notified, may be instanced as one of those ingenious persons, whose ecentricities were still more remarkable than their professional abilities, the memory of which extra circumstances have largely contributed to the perpetuation of their fame......It is not our intention to speak of the aberrations of men of genius with levity, but would rather advert [to] them, with commiseration and pity. Yet, to dwell upon the pursuits or to relate the opinions of such visionaries as the late Mr Blake with seriousness would be an attempt beyond the limits of our editorial gravity.

This was to be the English public's introduction to the genius who had been living and working in its midst. But abroad, *literati* fared - indeed already had fared - considerably better. Although he did not actually meet Blake until 1825 Henry Crabb Robinson is generally acknowledged as being the author of an article which appeared, in German, in the Hamburg periodical *Vaterländisches Museum* in 1811. Critically speaking it owed a good deal to some impressions of Blake which Benjamin Heath Malkin had published in his *A Father's Memoirs of His Child* five years before. It is prefaced with the Shakespearean couplet (quoted in English):

> The lunatic, the lover and the poet,
> Are of imagination all compact.

a perception which ought to have been enough in itself to forestall the fruitless torrent of speculation on Blake's sanity that has since followed. But the essay is of greatest interest for the excellent translations into German from the *Songs*, which were the work of a Dr Nikolaus Heinrich Julius. A single stanza from "The Tyger" shows how completely Julius assimilated Blake's spirit.

> Tiger, Tiger, Flammenpracht,
> In den Wäldern düstrer Nacht!

> Sprich, wess Gottes Aug und Hand,
> Dich so furchtbar schön verband?

Julius's rhythm and his concrete imagery catch the Blake unfalteringly throughout. Particularly remarkable is his rendering of the crux line of the poem:

> Did he who made the Lamb make thee?

as:

> Der das Lamb schuf, schuf er dich?

in which the concentration available to German grammar produces a version which is an honest rival to its original. Thus, almost a generation before London's salons had even learnt to to sneer at Blake, Germany had the opportunity to admire his unique power (as it had already learnt to love and admire Shakespeare through the fine translations of A. W. Schlegel).

But though the 'official' verdict on Blake was at the time of his death so negative, we have on record good opinions of him during his life from those whose good opinion was worth having. Coleridge had read the *Songs of Innocence and Experience* and, although he had his criticisms, was full of praise for much of the book. He described his first sensations in a letter to the Rev H. F. Cary: "I have this morning been reading a strange publication, viz poems with very wild and interesting pictures, as swathing/etched (I suppose) but it is said printed and painted by the author William Blake. He is a man of capital genius..." Thereafter he was evidently in Blake's company moderately often, although no chronicler has caught a word of what may have passed between them. We get only a tantalising glimpse of their affinity with each other in an anonymous essay on Blake in the *London University Magazine* of March 1830.

> Blake and Coleridge, when in company, seemed like congenial beings of another sphere, breathing for a while on our earth....

And the essayist remarks perceptively that had Blake lived in Germany he would by then have had his due recognition.

Two of the finest critics of the times, Lamb and Hazlitt, both held Blake in high regard. Lamb's verdict on the "The Tyger" was that it was a "glorious" work and that its author was "one of the most extraordinary persons of the age". On having some of the *Songs* read to him by Crabb Robinson, Hazlitt pronounced them "beautiful, and only too deep for the vulgar". But he added "He is ruined by vain struggles to get rid of what presses on his brain he attempts impossibles." This is an astute critique of Blake's peculiar type of creativity and of the dangers attending it.

I have not addressed the question of Blake's madness since it seems obvious that he was not mad. Unlike, say, Cowper he clearly suffered from no clinical condition. But creativity is a mysterious business. It cannot be legislated for. The prolonged strain of the intense discipline required to render imagination and vision coherent as art will throw off strange excrescences when the artist stands down for a moment from that daunting plane of existence. He may become absurd, crude, whimsical, childish, or even simply mundane. When an admirer introduced Joyce and Proust to each other and retired to be at a discreet distance from the terrific explosions of thought that must surely ensue from this momentous conjunction, the two great men exchanged a single, banal sentence with each other on the subject of truffles.

Like all supremely gifted artists Blake stood above his society and his age. He was a being to whom no corner of experience, physical, psychological or spiritual, was to be shut. This propensity may have led him into by-ways and up blind alleys. He sometimes threw in his own way huge crags he could not climb. But he never betrayed the reader by asking him to accept counterfeit coin as a substitute for the truth as he saw it.

As a man he retained to the end an extraordinary humility. He never acted the great sage. Though he could be dogmatic when pursued by trite cynicism into his spiritual heartlands, he found a continuing delight in discussing fresh ideas, especially in the company of the young.

We see him at the end, through the eyes of his young admirer Samuel Palmer, the one painter of his times whose vision could in some degree approach his own:

> He was one of the few to be met with in our passage through life who are not in some way "double minded" and inconsistent with themselves; one of the very few who cannot be depressed by neglect, and to whose name rank and station could add no lustre. Moving apart in the sphere above the attraction of worldly honours, he did not accept greatness, but confer it. He ennobled poverty and, by his conversation and the influence of his genius, made two small rooms in Fountain Court more attractive than the threshhold of princes.

That is, perhaps, the best epitaph for a man whose majestic nature was entirely of a piece with his art.

SELECT BIBLIOGRAPHY

EDITIONS:

The Complete Writings of William Blake edited by Geoffrey Keynes
(Oxford 1966)

Blake the Complete Poems edited by W. H. Stevenson,
(New York 1971)

The Illuminated Blake annotated by David Erdman
(New York 1974)

The Complete Poetry and Prose of William Blake edited by David V.
Erdman (New York 1988)

BIOGRAPHICAL/CRITICAL:

Alexander Gilchrist (revised D. G. Rossetti) *The Life of William Blake*
(1863, 1880)

W. B. Yeats Introduction to *Poems of William Blake* (1893)

Joseph Wicksteed *Blake's Vision of the Book of Job* (1910)

G. K. Chesterton *William Blake* (1910)

Mona Wilson *The Life of William Blake* (1927, 1948, 1971)

Northrop Frye *Fearful Symmetry* (1947)

David Erdman *Prophet Against Empire* (1954)

Anthony Blunt *The Art of William Blake* (1959)

Peter F. Fisher *The Valley of Vision* (1961)

Harold Bloom *Blake's Apocalypse* (1963)

Bernard Blackstone *English Blake* (1966)

G. E. Bentley, Jr *Blake Records* (1969)
and *Blake Records Supplement* (1988)

S. Foster Damon *A Blake Dictionary* (1973)

E. P. Thompson *Witness Against The Beast* (1993)

Peter Ackroyd *Blake* (1995)